AGE
YOUR
WAY

Create a Unique Legacy

DEBBIE PEARSON, RN

FAMILY NIGHT PRESS
www.FamilyNightPress.com

FAMILY NIGHT PRESS
AUSTIN·TEXAS
www.FamilyNightPress.com

ISBN 978-0-9978533-0-8 (paperback)
ISBN 978-0-9978533-2-2 (ePUB)
ISBN 978-0-9978533-3-9 (mobi)
Library of Congress Control Number: 2016911780

Publishing manager: Janica Smith, *www.PublishingSmith.com*
Copyeditor: Lisa Canfield, *www.copycoachlisa.com*
Indexer: Elena Gwynn, *www.quillandinkindexing.com*
Cover and interior design by Monica Thomas for TLC Graphics,
www.TLCGraphics.com

Printed in the United States of America

DEDICATION

To the patients, families, and caregivers who
touched my heart and provided the
stories to tell.

To my family who are beyond a dream come true
for a mother and grandmother.

To Hank, my husband, my soulmate, my heartbeat.
You fill my heart with love and joy every day.

TABLE of CONTENTS

CHAPTER ONE

Control or No Control

It's Your Decision

You wouldn't go on a trip without a plan: Tickets, agenda, a place to stay, gas in the car, reservations, maybe even some research on where you're going. Yet, for our most mysterious and complicated journey, the one that begins with age or injury, most of us are like hitchhikers on a deserted road. We jump into a stranger's car and, before we know it, we're swerving around a bend toward an eighteen-wheeler and we realize our driver is drunk and the seatbelt doesn't work, and...

Don't be that traveler.

Instead, realize your own extraordinary aging journey can last years, even decades, with twists, turns and surprises around every corner. This book's purpose is to help you survey the terrain, design your own map, and *age your way*. Its customizable lessons apply whether you're looking ahead to your own future or scrambling to assist an elderly relative or a family member in crisis.

If you haven't planned, you're in good company. Our society seldom applauds life's final act; everyone knows what's next, so let's all cover our eyes. But denial not only diminishes the last third of our excellent adventure in this world, it puts somebody else in the driver's seat—a sure way to hit that oncoming truck.

We can do better. Think about how enthusiastically you prepared for other milestones: Higher education, career, parenting. We study, focus, and try to guide the course of our lives. I've learned you can draw upon the same skills for the aging years with rewarding results.

With this book as your guide, your personal plan will leave no question about your unique wishes for both living and dying; more than that, your plan will include legal and financial information that will be essential to executing your strategy. When shared, your written plan will provide a gift to your family, saving them from the agony of choosing for you while they fight with each other over who can better read your mind. Documentation is crucial, since with aging or injury, there is a chance you won't be able to verbally communicate your wishes or be actively involved with decision-making. If that time comes, what's in writing must serve as your voice.

By sharing patient stories and hands-on experience, I'll introduce you to the benefit of applying control to the aging process to avoid the heartbreak that comes from lack of planning. So whether you are elderly or a supportive family member, you'll find there is much to be gleaned by reading on.

Starting out as a new nurse, I believed my patients' greatest concern was physical pain. But that turned out to be wrong. In four decades at the bedsides of thousands of patients, I've learned that a single fear exceeds all others: The fear of losing control. Yet those of us who do not make a conscious decision *for* control will inevitably default to no control. I've seen what "no control" looks like time and again as a nurse and patient advocate. As an intensive care nurse, I've felt the crack of breaking ribs under my hands when resuscitating a ninety-year-old frail lady whose weight matched her years. Could this possibly be what she wanted?

Debbie – a newly minted, bright-eyed Registered Nurse in 1978

All of my patients—those who seized control and those who lacked it—have inspired and informed this book. I'm grateful to be able to share their stories. With their help, I offer options to everyone brave enough to take the needed steps.

Out of the hundreds of stories that demonstrate the elusive rascal that is control, I'll start with one that involves my own mother, Mimi. At eighty-four, Mimi fell at home, resulting in both a stroke and a hip fracture. There was no advance plan in place and no preference documented, because Mimi was not one to talk about three things: weight, aging, or death. I never knew whether she considered that kind of discussion disagreeable or simply rude, but these topics were banned. Her silence relinquished control to family.

Without any direction from Mimi, my father (Papa) and I became joint decision makers. This was natural for Papa, as he had already assumed many of Mimi's responsibilities because of a situation both parents had decided to ignore: Mimi had been experiencing dementia for years. I remember my silent relief as the truth I had long suspected was revealed. Through a series of questions, the hospital neurologist finally brought dementia into the light for Papa. To establish a baseline of information, the doctor asked Papa who did the grocery shopping, the cooking, the laundry, the driving. Papa proudly admitted to doing it all. The physician then asked who had been managing these tasks ten years ago. *Mimi.* Her dementia became a reality.

Immediate decisions in the hospital were complicated. Mimi was confused, couldn't walk, couldn't swallow. In instances of no written direction, hospital protocol is to follow all procedures medically indicated, and this was the situation with Mimi. It was also what Papa wanted: Whatever it took to keep the love of his life with him. Without a surgically placed feeding tube directly into the stomach, Mimi would not have survived. She got a new hip, artificial nutrition, and a rehabilitation plan. Each step after surgery was torture. Motivating a confused, frail lady to take a painful step forward took an army of cheerleaders. She could not comprehend what we were asking, but she did respond to the cheers and hugs—so progress was made, one inch at a time. Papa became an expert at tube feedings and I learned an assortment of swallow therapies. Within six months, Mimi regained her ability to swallow and the feeding tube was removed. She learned to use a walker and used it when she remembered. A new normal was established.

Papa was a devoted caregiver. He'd worked in his own men's clothing store until the age of eighty and still had a great deal of energy. The decision was made to refocus his energy from that of a merchant to being a full-time care provider. He saw no point in hiring caregivers for Mimi and simply took her around like a child. To my horror, he also left her home alone when he had errands to do. Papa and I disagreed vehemently about his obligation to her safety. I even threatened to report him to Adult Protective Services if he continued to leave her unsupervised. This got me absolutely nowhere. His solution was both stubborn and effective. He would lean Mimi back in her recliner and close her hand around a

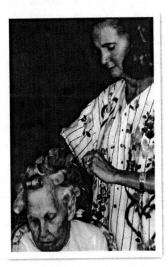

Spa Day – Debbie fixing Mimi's hair

note that read, "Don't get out of the chair. I will be back home soon." Remarkably, since she was still able to read, this plan worked. Mimi never had a fall (to my knowledge) when she was by herself.

Time went on, with Papa managing Mimi in a manner that didn't crimp his active lifestyle. My sister and I helped when needed. A couple of years into his caregiving role, Papa decided Mimi would be easier to manage if he cut her hair like a man's; goodbye beauty shop. I protested. I knew my fashionable mother too well to accept this solution. So we set up a "spa day" where I would treat her to a shampoo, hair styling, nails, skin care, the works. On one of the days, at the end of the spa routine, my mother took my face in her freshly manicured hands, smiled her beautiful smile, and asked me, "Does your mother know where you are?"

When Mimi's front tooth fell out (as often happens with aging), Papa wheeled her around to show her off. He'd never known her as a child and now, to his delight, she looked just like an adorable six-year-old. His sentiments were endearing, but I knew my mother. Again, she would have been appalled. We had the tooth replaced. Everything was a negotiation.

One enormous negotiation occurred when Papa wanted to vacation outside the country. By then, Mimi was below ninety pounds and had severe osteoporosis. I was happy to stay with Mimi, but I was not happy with the possibility of having to perform CPR (cardio-pulmonary-resuscitation) in case of emergency: One chest compression and her frail ribs would be broken in pieces. Papa at first refused to sign the required form that would protect Mimi from chest compressions. After all, she had given us no direction regarding CPR. Papa had to make this weighty decision on his own. I would not agree to keep Mimi unless he relented. Before he left on his trip, he signed the form.

About five years into Papa's caregiver tenure, Mimi got pneumonia. Clearly, it was time to talk about the inevitable fork in the road. For health changes, would we go the route of hospitalization or palliative care at home? I was sad that Mimi couldn't tell us what she wanted, but the whole family believed she'd prefer to stay in her own house. The

Mimi & Papa, the later years

family shuddered at the word *"hospice."* Did that mean she was about to die? No, it meant we would treat all conditions at home and focus on her comfort. There would be no more hospitalizations. Papa decided against antibiotics, but wanted to know what could be done to help her body naturally resolve the pneumonia. We increased her fluids, kept Mimi sitting up and taking deep breaths as much of the day as her little body could tolerate. It worked. The pneumonia resolved and Mimi remained under hospice care for a year and a half.

The hardest time of all came when Mimi lost her ability to swallow completely, as is typical in end-stage dementia. Papa had been so dedicated to preparing her favorite foods and keeping her healthy that initially he felt that he had failed. Eventually, he put her to bed for the last time and told her she was going to have the big sleep. That is how she died, peacefully in her sleep.

Mimi's story unfolded naturally and concluded with our closely connected family more bonded than ever. We had no guide, but we were like-minded, a rarity. We were able to negotiate with elasticity and arrive at the end free of emotional injury.

However, I have witnessed too many situations where this isn't the case. Disagreement and oppositional values are prevalent in our fragmented society. Generations no longer live in the same house, same city, or same state. Growing apart and developing our own unique set of beliefs has become the norm. A single son working a farm is unlikely to have the same framework for decision making as his married city sister with three children. Simply being born to the same parents does not guarantee like values. Then, why not let the patient guide the course? That is the mantra of Age Your Way: Discuss, document, share the information, and do it early while you still can. Letting the patient set their own course places a layer of protection over the family.

⌐ LESSON ⌐

Ideally, choices about your living and dying belong with only one person: You. Anyone approaching the elderly years is ripe to execute a written plan for this stage. Done right, it not only protects you, it also protects your family from painful decisions and unpleasant disputes. Implementing control becomes an act of love.

Any reason to delay?

Read on to learn about the three stages of life where you can control your choices. Every one of you will fit into one of these stages.

CHAPTER TWO

The Three Stages of Age Your Way

*If I Had Known I Was Going to Live So Long,
I Would Have Gotten Younger Friends*

Because of economic prosperity, many Americans have come to expect control over nearly every aspect of life. We control the temperature of our home and our car to within a degree of our ideal comfort range. We control our coffee to an absurd extent. We control the ring tone of our phone and choose from more than a hundred television channels. Doesn't it make sense to control the years ahead in case we won't be able to make our voice heard?

That time may come when we are old, or it may happen much sooner. Through unexpected illness or injury, rapid aging can hit our body like a speeding car. Aging is not necessarily chronological. Depending on your situation, you have three possibilities for controlling your aging plan.

As you read through the definitions and examples of each, try to mentally put yourself in the place of the patient. It will help you understand the three stages.

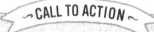

~CALL TO ACTION~

Everyone has three possible options for planning; each of us will fall into one of these stages. Which fits you or your loved one?

- **Stage One** is where *you* are in control of planning. Mental clarity and the ability to follow a structured format are needed. When planning in this stage is completed, it represents an accurate reflection of your wishes.

- **Stage Two** requires *assistance* for planning. These individuals may have been reluctant to plan, in denial, or simply unaware. They can still express their wishes and provide information. However, they no longer have the ability or energy to keep the planning process moving forward. Guidance is required to extract their wishes and other pertinent information. The person assisting them — maybe that's you — performs the gathering and documentation. Done right, the completed plan is still an accurate reflection of the person's wishes.

- **Stage Three** is where someone else does the best they can to *handle your crisis*. Ability to state your wishes may be limited or completely absent. Gathering data is tortuous and frequently erroneous. Vital pieces of the puzzle are often missing. The plan may not reflect who you are and what you want. Personal control is lost.

BILL: AGING *HIS* WAY
(STAGE ONE)

Years ago, I assisted an engineer who, at 47, received a dev-astating diagnosis: Huntington's disease. This is an inherited condition that causes progressive degeneration of nerve cells in the brain, affecting muscle coordination, mental ability, and behavioral symptoms. To compound the tragedy, his two teenage daughters stood a fifty-fifty chance of inheriting the congenital disorder, making this a family crisis.

On meeting Bill, I recognized his intelligence, strength, and compassion for others, all of which stoked his decision to make a plan immediately. Like the best of plans, this was an act of love. Still, following his diagnosis, his marriage dissolved, as is often the case with catastrophic conditions. His daughters operated in a state of fear for both their father and their future.

Bill knew three things for certain: The disease would end his life, he wanted to spare his young daughters from burdensome responsibility, and he needed to make a plan to guide the stages of his illness. He got busy on our Age Your Way plan, documenting all his wishes and assigning medical and financial powers of attorney to his brother, a decision designed to relieve pressure on his girls and to assure his wishes were followed. Special documents protected Bill's financial assets for his minor daughters, using government benefits where possible. Because Bill's brother lived out of state, he engaged me to oversee medical care as the disease progressed.

I began to work with Bill when he was in a retirement community that provided limited assistance. Bill was still independent at first but, when he lost the use of his arms, there was no option but to transfer to a skilled nursing facility. This is where he remained for three years and became both immobile and non-verbal. Nevertheless, we made decisions based on Bill's own wishes, communicated when he had a voice. When painful decision points were encountered, his brother and daughters did not need to wrestle with choices. Although silent, his voice was heard, his wishes followed. No guilt, no arguments. Bill controlled the outcome and minimized surprises. Everyone knew and honored his wishes for a natural death, daughters by his side.

It took a combination of inner strength, love, time, and structure to cover the multitude of requirements, but the effort was invaluable for all parties. Comprehensive pre-planning steps were considered—legal, financial, personal, and medical. These were clearly documented and communicated in family meetings. This is an ideal Stage One plan. Unfortunately, Bill is in the minority. Less than one-third of Americans have even executed documents to name their Power of Attorney or document their Directive to Physician.

STAGE 1: LESSON

Accelerated aging can happen at any chronological age. Do you have a plan in place if your life changed today? Is there any reason for you to wait?

PHYLLIS: DRUGS AND ALCOHOL
(STAGE TWO)

Working with Phyllis revealed that significant health issues don't have to rob a patient of their zest for life. Phyllis remained energetic and interesting, despite being physically disabled and in constant pain. After more than six back surgeries, metal structures held her spine together from neck to tailbone. Still she managed to have fun, walk, and stay active with the combination of her strong will, Oxycodone, and Hydrocodone. Phyllis was determined to live her life as she always had, and refused to take to her bed except to sleep at night.

However, there was a problem. Her routine included scotch and wine every evening. Her adult children were appalled and appropriately worried when they realized Phyllis considered cocktail hour to be non-negotiable. They knew mixing high-dose prescription narcotics and high-volume liquor was a recipe for trouble. Mother and children were at an impasse. The children held the official power of attorney and argued that Phyllis was impaired. They were ready to exert their authority. Phyllis was in that grey area of Stage Two—not fully capable mentally and physically, but not incapacitated.

Both Phyllis and her children put on their boxing gloves, ready for the fight. Neither side was willing to budge. I became the referee. As is typical with mediation, the only viable solution was a compromise. We sought a middle ground: A spot where Phyllis was free to continue her zest for life along with some peace of mind for her children. Against her will, Phyllis agreed to have a night sitter come to her home in time for cocktail hour each evening and remain with her until morning. Against their better judgment, the family agreed to accommodate her life of prescription drugs and alcohol. This mediated plan went on for four years—and it worked. When the end came for Phyllis, it was unrelated to narcotics or alcohol. It was from an overwhelming infection in her spine. She'd been permitted to live her life her way until the end.

⁓STAGE 2: LESSON⁓

Collaboration is key. The plan is the patient's plan, based on what provides *that* person quality of life. Support people are engaged to understand the patient's wishes, gather information, document, and execute the patient's plan. This is not an opportunity to change lifelong habits and wishes, but to serve as an extension of that person. Isn't that what you would want and deserve?

CONNIE: WHAT DID YOU REALLY WANT?
(STAGE THREE)

Connie had progressive dementia. Although her life had been good in ways, she also had heartaches that left her alone. Her only child, a daughter, had died at thirty from cancer, and Connie then lost her husband to a heart attack when they were both in their fifties. Once alone, Connie remained in her home for a quarter century, settled into an independent yet solitary routine that was successful until she was in her eighties. Determined to protect her financial resources, she began hiding her checkbooks in safe places, so safe that Connie herself couldn't find them. Week after week, she would walk on her own to the neighborhood bank, order more checks, and withdraw twenty-five dollars in cash. Eventually, the bank teller became concerned and called me to do a home evaluation.

Connie had clearly retained her social skills and we talked about the special way she made deviled eggs for university parties. However, she was unable to provide her date of birth, social security number, the name of a single contact person, or any health history. She had long ago stopped seeing her doctor or taking any of her medications. Unopened prescriptions from five years ago were neatly lined up on her kitchen windowsill. Her weight had dropped to under a hundred pounds and there was very little food in the home, only apples and Raisin Bran. Her higher-level executive functioning was long gone.

We worked together for twelve years, but I was never able to extract Connie's priorities or her wishes for future planning. Nobody was available to help me understand who Connie was so that I could tailor a plan that was truly hers. Would Connie want everything done medically? Did she have religious beliefs that should be considered? What I knew was that she chose to remain in her home, wanted her financial resources preserved, and that she gravitated toward a solitary existence. That became the plan of care, to perpetuate her quiet home environment until the end of her days. The rest of her plan was all conjecture.

How I wish it were different. How I wanted to know more as one year turned to another. Would she choose a feeding tube, CPR, dialysis? My heart ached for her inability to tell me what she wanted. As a result, decisions were made that were a middle-of-the-road compromise. We treated what was relatively simple, avoiding anything that would cause her undue pain or distress. I still worry about what choices were right and what may have been wrong for Connie as an individual.

One thing that Connie shared with me early on still stays in my memory. She told me, "If I had known I was going to live so long, I would have gotten younger friends."

> ⌐ STAGE 3: LESSON ⌐
>
> Begin your plan early. Identify someone younger to be responsible for executing your plan. If you have aging parents, encourage them to share their wishes before they enter Stage Three. A unique form of closeness comes from sharing who you are and what you want.

Now that you understand the three stages, let's move on and look at ways you can find and record your voice. We'll look at how things used to be, today's reality, and how you can protect both you and those you love by putting a plan in place for the future.

CHAPTER THREE

Find Your Voice

Grandma Is Going to the Hospital for a "Family Vacation"

The 2010 Census Bureau grouped the elderly into three sub-populations due to tremendous growth in that demographic. We now have the "young old" (sixty-five to seventy-four), the "old" (seventy-five to eighty-four) and the "oldest old" (eighty-five plus). The growth rate of the oldest old is twice that of those sixty-five and over and almost four times that of the total population. These rapidly expanding populations impact all our lives, current and future.

As I write this, the oldest old are those who lived through the hardships of World War II and the Great Depression. Despite their strength and resilience, they chose to surrender their health care management to the "all-knowing" doctor. There was no authorization required for invasive procedures, no forms to sign for release of medical information, and health care was inexpensive. I worked with this group during the 1970s when their parents were aging. They could admit their frail elderly family member to the hospital with no diagnosis other than "family vacation." There was absolutely no reason to worry about Grandma while away having fun. For the current oldest old, hospitals were an ideal solution for care and feeding of the aging or incapacitated. No questions asked, no worries, just entrust management to the doctor.

Of course, in the 1970s, the doctor who was treating you was likely to really know you. As a matter of fact, he (rarely *she*) may have known you your whole life. He knew your family and what you did for a living. Everyone assumed he knew your values, and knew how you would have wanted to be treated. And if treatment ended up being inconsistent with patient wishes, no one questioned it. In fact, no one consulted the patient about his or her wishes, so it was a moot issue. The doctor had all the information, and could be trusted with all decisions.

Fast forward to the jigsaw puzzle of today's medical system, in which typically no single doctor is in charge of your treatment. If fortunate, you have a primary care physician in the community who knows *something* about you. But this doctor is only one piece of the puzzle and his or her involvement ends at the hospital door. At the hospital, multiple specialists treat one part of you, but not the whole. The final piece of the puzzle is the hospital-based doctor (the "hospitalist") who treats all of you, but only in the hospital. The best you can hope for is that all of these puzzle pieces at least touch.

Of course, critical decisions often must be made when the patient is compromised and unable to provide input and process complex thoughts. The fortunate patients have loving family or a close friend to assist in their time of need. Today, however, without all the proper legal documents, family and friends can receive no medical information about you and can make no decisions. Should the hospital adhere strictly to the letter of the law, even a spouse may be unable to access medical information without the right paperwork. Remember, without authorized direction to the contrary, the medical system is obligated to follow all procedures medically indicated. Control is in the hands of medical practitioners who do not know you. Together we'll look at how the current system impacts patients and families.

The stories I share throughout this book are all true and come directly from my forty-year nursing career. I have changed patient names for privacy. In 2000, I founded a company called Nurses Case Management (NCM). After more than 20 years of hospital and home health nursing, NCM was my way of meeting patient needs that fell through the cracks of the health care system. The mission of my case management company was to put the patient first and serve as their advocate. In this role, my patients and their families have taught me more than I could have ever imagined. What a gift.

Over time, NCM evolved beyond case management and also accepted the role of court-appointed guardian for individuals. Most families never need to go through the legal guardianship process. The vast majority of aging parents receive support from their family as a unit. However, not everyone is so fortunate. That is where NCM came in as a court-appointed guardian, tasked with discerning the wishes of incapacitated individuals, adhering to ethical guidelines that put the patient's needs first. The following story of Donald is an example of the need for guardianship.

Donald was beginning to warm to the idea of planning for his future. Opening up was difficult for him as he was a private man, divorced, and estranged from his only daughter. His sole contacts were a housekeeper and one friend. At our initial meeting, Donald made it clear that he wanted no contact with his daughter. Whatever had transpired between the two of them was irreparable.

Suddenly, Donald had a massive stroke. Decisions needed to be made and time was of the essence, but no legal papers were in place. Because Donald was unresponsive and without a voice, it was too late for him to execute legal documents. His estranged daughter at first attempted to insert herself, but quickly backed out when it became clear she would need to become his court-appointed guardian, subject to screening and reporting requirements. NCM became his guardian.

However, we had not known Donald long, certainly not long enough to look through his eyes in making decisions. Ethically, the only way to proceed was to interview the few people who knew him—his ex-wife, his housekeeper, and his only friend. Fortunately, everyone concurred that his past behavior indicated he would opt for palliative care instead of life support. He was placed on hospice services, provided with one-on-one care to assure his comfort, and died a peaceful and dignified death. We will never know if this was the right decision for Donald as he surrendered all control because he did not plan.

Donald's decision-making situation is not the norm, but neither is it rare. Families are often scattered and children are reunited with parents at a time where little to no information is available. It may be too late to learn more in some instances, or there is no attempt at a deeper understanding. Even families who are physically close may not have explored beneath superficial conversation.

Traditional parent-child patterns may continue into adulthood until a crisis hits. How much do children know their parents as individuals with unique needs, wishes, and fears? During a recent meeting to document one woman's priorities and preferences for care so her children would have a guide for decision making, the patient looked me straight in the eyes and said with clarity, "My children have no idea who I am." I wonder how true this is for a significant percentage of the population. Regardless of your age, it is time to plan for yourself and create a written guide for those you love to follow.

~ LESSON ~

There is no way to know when you will be unable to speak for yourself. It can happen suddenly. If you have no plan in place, you have no control. Put it in writing to avoid confusion from misinterpretation or memory lapses.

The written plan I developed is found in *The Blueprint to Age Your Way*. It evolved gradually as I witnessed anxiety from lack of planning and absence of critical information. Patients taught me much regarding what is needed and propelled me to develop a structure aimed at being proactive. All generations may find this useful as it can be developed at any of the three stages: Stage One (total control), Stage Two (with collaboration), or Stage Three (crisis management). *The Blueprint to Age Your Way* is my solution. There may be other options available for you to utilize. What matters is that you give the gift of knowledge to your family.

Information is power, as the adage goes. Some want to hold on to information as a means of retaining authority over the situation. However, that strategy morphs to a lack of control during injury or aging. When you need help the most, do you want family making panicked decisions in the dark? Of course not. You also don't want them spending months digging through piles of trash and treasure to figure out the puzzle of your life and your medical wishes.

After a career of helping families painfully excavate health-related preferences as well as legal and financial data, I decided to develop a blueprint to simplify the process and consolidate information. When I committed to make this a reality, the goal was my number one New Year's Resolution. To assure this became a truly useful tool, I decided to try it out first on my husband Hank and myself. The concept was imbedded in my mind, but required structure. To my great surprise, it took the better part of a year to extract and organize every detail of our lives, as I had never looked at all the different pieces as a whole. At times, it felt like nailing Jell-O to the wall. The minute I thought I had one area covered, it would only raise another question. The work was slow and frustrating at intervals. But I wanted the flow of the blueprint to be orderly and comprehensive so I kept on with the task until it was finished. When completed, we had a compilation of health-related desires, contacts in our lives, legal documents, financial data, and more.

The following January, Hank and I sat down with our three adult children and their three spouses for a family meeting. This was an adult gathering, none of the eight grandchildren were allowed. We reviewed each chapter as our children sat in silence (a rarity for them). When finished, we looked up to see tears of appreciation in the eyes of all. With the realization that they would not have to sort through chaos when we needed help, they were grateful beyond words. It was at that moment I realized this gift was ready for the giving to others.

This is one of the actual family meetings to update our "Age Your Way Plan."
It has become an annual event, as the plan changes a little each year.
At the end of this book, I'll list the order of the planning blueprint
so you'll understand the process better.

~ EXERCISE ~

Close your eyes and imagine your family sitting together to find out more about you, your priorities, plans, wishes, finances, legal documents, and much more. What kind of relief would this provide to both them and you? It's all possible.

CHAPTER FOUR

Special Dispensation for Dementia

The Beauty of Retrogrowth

It would be a shame not to include my father's unique name for dementia: *"Retrogrowth, a growing backwards mentally to compensate for the trauma of being inside a body that is dying."* He experienced my mother's dementia as a gift, his chance to be with her as a fresh and beautiful child, unconcerned with social pressure or responsibility. It was a precious time when responsibility to family and work disappeared. They were able

Mimi and Papa on their wedding day

to simply be a couple and they became closer than they had ever been.

Unlike my parents' experience, many stories of dementia are neither happy nor beautiful. The veneer of social correctness can be stripped away as people with dementia lose control over their words and actions. This can injure those around them, invoking hurt and negative reactions. Formerly fragile relationships can fracture beyond repair. Sadly, when these people need support and love the most, their indiscriminate words and deeds can repel their loved ones. Monumental challenges flourish as filters evaporate. The colossal challenge for loved ones: Remember it's not personal. Bad behavior and angry words reflect the illness, not the patient, and certainly not the family member. The disease is talking. Depending on what part of the brain is affected, you might see lashing-out as never before. Again, this is not a deliberate act. To expect someone with advanced dementia to choose their words carefully would be as fruitless as asking a one-armed man to clap his hands.

In working with families, I look at the loss of J-I-M: Judgment, insight, and memory. Remember J-I-M when you are working with dementia patients, as logical discussions become futile. It will help you recognize what is gone and more accurately set realistic expectations. One of my favorite patients was a six-foot-three-inch handsome man with the distinguished look of a movie star. I loved taking him to doctor appointments because I could count on lively and interactive discussions. However, over time, his filters faded and he lost judgment concerning what he should or should not say aloud. For example, one day, we sat in a large clinic's waiting room and, in his booming voice, he asked me, "Why is everyone in health care so fat?"

⌐ LESSON ⌐

Nothing about dementia is deliberate. It is a medical condition, out of control. When J-I-M (judgment, insight, memory) is gone, recognize how little is left for reasoning.

From the onset, those who have a loved one with dementia can benefit enormously from an Alzheimer's support group, regardless of the formal diagnosis. Dementia is not a disease, but a symptom seen in many disorders including Alzheimer's, Parkinson's, stroke, and others. The Alzheimer's Association has become the umbrella organization for dementia awareness and assistance, so they typically coordinate the list and location of group meetings. Don't get stuck on the term "Alzheimer's" if your loved one has a different illness or circumstance. All dementia-causing diseases share a common thread of care and management.

The average survival time for people exhibiting dementia is about four and a half years. Those diagnosed before age seventy typically live a decade or longer. The marathon nature of this condition cries out for ongoing support, not merely from family and friends but from others walking the same path. You will benefit in a variety of ways from a support group, as the attendees will become your smartest friends. Professionals can assist with planning and major decisions. But your support group will be indispensable when it comes to everyday challenges.

For both emotional and financial reasons, families typically care for loved ones with dementia at home. However, these family members (usually spouses or children) often continue caregiving long past the time they can physically and emotionally manage the work. To successfully keep your loved one at home for as long as possible, it helps to acknowledge from the start that you cannot do it alone. It is imperative that you schedule some time every week for yourself, free of caregiving duties. Ask a friend or family member to pitch in. Look to the options of a paid attendant or respite day-out program, which are typically affordable part-time options. Back-up care is not only right for you, it's right for your loved one, enabling some degree of flexibility, which may prove necessary. What if you have to go to the hospital, attend a funeral or simply want to visit your grandchildren? Your loved one won't be devastated by your absence if he or she is already used to someone else. Consider this sobering statistic: Those caring for someone with dementia have a thirty percent chance of dying first. Preparation is key.

Should care in the home cease to be an option, let me walk you through the steps of facility placement. This can be one of the most gut-wrenching decisions you will ever make. But that doesn't mean it's the wrong decision. Transition to a care facility is intended to put your loved one in the hands of experienced caregivers, arriving fresh each shift. After placement, you are allowed to resume the simpler but irreplaceable role of family.

So, what is involved? First the bad news. Most dementia facilities are costly and not covered by insurance, although government funding may be available for some. At the time this book was written, national cost averages were between thirty-two-hundred and fifty-eight-hundred dollars per month, with some considerably more expensive. In the

U.S., more is spent on dementia care than on heart disease and cancer care combined. With millions of aging baby boomers in the population, this statistic will only worsen.

Whether you're considering care outside the home in the immediate future or putting it off until some future date, the earlier you start your search the better. The best facility for your loved one may not be immediately available. You may need to get on the waiting list for an indeterminate period of time. Step one in the process is to locate facility options from your doctor, a professional consultant, your support group, or a friend. The price of a consultant may seem daunting on top of all the other expenses, but it may save you in the long run. This is a big decision and you may find it worthwhile to pay for *unbiased* advice. If using a consultant, be sure to ask if he or she receives a *finder's fee* for the facility.

⌐ EXERCISE ↶

1. List three qualities that would give you confidence in a dementia care facility.

2. Maintain a list of facilities you hear mentioned, with comments for each, good and bad. Note the source and contact. (This list will be useful if the need for placement comes up suddenly. You want to be prepared with a written list when you are pressured to act at a time when emotions may undermine logic.)

3. For every "good" facility on your list, make a phone call. Ask if there is a waiting list, and what the length of the wait is usually. Depending on the answer, you may want to get your loved one on the list right at that moment.

Once you have recommendations for a facility, the next step is a tour. In looking at the facility, do NOT consider the chandelier or the artwork as these will deliver no care. Instead, look at the patients. Is someone interacting with them? Are they involved in activities? Do the patients appear clean and happy? Make sure the place feels cozy enough to become your loved one's home. It should have on-site medical management by physicians and other providers. Close proximity to where you live also holds a tremendous benefit. When nearby, you can easily handle oversight and quickly respond to problems.

Once you've chosen your loved one's new home, it's time to focus on making a smooth transition. That will be possible only if you convey information about your loved one in advance of moving day. Share every detail you can think of, especially about what calms your family member, as well as his or her interests, favorite foods and possible negative triggers. Advance knowledge is key to success.

Some facilities allow day programs in advance of move-in, so your loved one will become familiar with the layout, atmosphere, and staff. When this is not an option, arrange to have belongings transferred to the patient's room prior to placement. This is minimally a two-person job. Your loved one should not participate in the move process and should be away from the house while personal items are relocated. Realize that items you move are at risk to disappear so don't bring anything that has high value, either emotionally or financially. Residents "share" each other's possessions, so you may see your mother's favorite purse being carried by someone else and your mother may be wearing the other woman's dress. The sharing goes both directions and random distribution of goods is common.

When the facility room appears home-like, it's time to move in. You may want to remain for the first evening through dinner, and visit with others in the community. When the moment comes to leave, give assurances you'll return but don't linger. Staff should be available to distract your loved one as you depart, since a prolonged or emotional goodbye serves more to upset than to soothe. The goal is to transition dependence to the hands-on staff. I know that sounds painful but it's important. You want dementia-trained workers, fresh with each shift, to provide the medical and personal care—while you continue as a loving family member, a role that never changes. It does take time to regain your emotional footing after the move and to abandon feelings of guilt. But, time and again, I've seen family caregivers replace torment with contentment as they replenish their bodies and brains with needed rest. And that's the good news.

I recall so clearly the situation with Maggie. She was in a general assisted-living center, continually anxious, always a mess, and never receiving enough personal attention. However, moving her to a dementia facility meant a more restrictive care environment and locked doors. It was a difficult decision, but necessary as she was failing at a precipitous rate. The move was made and Maggie was put in a hospice program. All expectations were that a rapid decline and death would follow soon. Quite the contrary. Maggie regained strength, made friends, ate, and even gained a boyfriend. She was among staff who anticipated her needs, understood dementia protocols, and protected her when afraid. It was the right move for her.

Another dementia-related consideration that takes insight to comprehend is a phenomenon I call *time travel*. Your loved one with dementia will mentally re-experience a variety of life stages as their condition progresses. You may be shocked to realize that you have become obsolete in his or her life. For example, when my own mother cognitively returned to her childhood, why would she need a husband? Ridiculous! And of course, I had to accept that she couldn't have had a daughter, because she viewed herself as a child. When your loved one time-travels, you must eliminate your own sensitivities and accept the mental stage in which your loved one is living. When she cries out for her mother who has been dead for fifty years, be the understudy and step in as a mother. When she is holding hands and flirting with another man while still married to you, don't take it personally. It's part of the time journey that can be fun or scary. Keep your focus on meeting her needs. This time journey with your loved one can be scary or unsettling, but can also be enjoyable and enlightening. After all, it's a unique opportunity for you to appreciate more years of his or her life in *Retrogrowth*.

In the next chapter, you'll find a story I was hesitant to share.

CHAPTER FIVE

No Option for Collaboration

A Choice

As painful as this chapter is to write, it is necessary. It's the story of my father's aging and his choices. He died in August of 2010 at the age of ninety-one, three years after the death of my mother from Alzheimer's. We had always been close, both emotionally and geographically, as our homes were less than a mile apart. A trim and active man, his greatest joy came from living life to the fullest and interacting with others, whether a door-to-door salesman or a state senator. Any kind of face-to-face discussion with another person was a good interaction for him. At the age of eighty, he closed down his men's clothing store to become a full-time caregiver for my mother. If she hadn't needed care, there's no telling how long he would have kept working. Even after working, he kept his little red calendar in his shirt pocket, filled with appointments and social activities. As a well-read and intelligent man, he could talk on any subject. As a community philanthropist, he touched many lives in our town of Austin. As an author, he wrote small books every year, printed three hundred copies for his closest friends, and hand-delivered them. It was his way of sharing thoughts and staying in touch. Some writings bordered on profound, others were quirky and written only to instigate controversy. All were unedited.

Papa volunteering at the Alzheimer's program.
Little red calendar book in his shirt pocket.

Up until the moment Papa died, he was a shining light in any room, mentally sharp; he drove his little white car with crank windows and lived independently in his own house. Donating his free hours to the Alzheimer's Day Out Program was one of his most gratifying activities. He kept it up even after my mother died, volunteering the last time just days before his own death. He loved people and they loved him, a remarkable and admired gentleman.

Behind the scenes, it was my responsibility to keep him safe and sound. This was no easy task as he preferred to talk his body into healing rather than go to the doctor. He also talked to God and said *she* was very good at providing answers. Within reason, he would allow me to accompany him to a few doctor appointments and accepted some basic heart medications. When he started having angina, he agreed to take Nitroglycerine to alleviate the chest pain.

As much as he cherished his large family and interpersonal relationships, Papa also cherished his autonomy. He never had a desire to control anyone else, but he had a fierce need to control himself, both in mind and body. For that reason, he took his own life while still independent and in control. The start of his suicide note read:

"Debbie just called. She is checking on me. What a dear. She wants to take care of me in my declining days. It is inconsiderate on my part to deprive her of what she does so well. She has been taking care of me for years now."

Although my mind understood his choice, my heart was angry at a level I had never before experienced. My father had killed himself! A knife in my chest would have hurt less. As the first family member on the scene, I received the interrogation from the homicide detective. Had my father ever mentioned suicide? What did I do about the discussion? The pain and anger deepened as I notified the rest of the family, made funeral arrangements, and administered the estate.

One of the most painful tasks came from a "to do" note he left for me. He had ordered a set of drums for the Alzheimer's Day Out Program, knowing the *friends* would get great joy from banging on the drums. They would not arrive at the music store until after his death. This was a task he left for me to do the week after his suicide. The cocktail of anger and nausea overtook me as I did what a good daughter would do—I picked up the drum set and delivered them to *Circle of Friends*. In hindsight, it was too soon, too personal, too traumatic. I wanted to throw the drums out a window.

Yes, Papa had both talked and written about choosing the time and manner of his death. We had these discussions for over thirty years. Everyone in the family was anaesthetized to the subject as he took such joy in being controversial. It was talk, not action. Until it was reality.

Years passed before I could make myself go back and read excerpts from his diary, written days before his death. Finally, my peace came from the understanding that this act was not about any of us left behind; it was about him and him alone. In his words:

"It is all a matter of control. I feel that my body has created me to help make decisions that will maximize the pleasure and minimize the pain that my body experiences on its journey from one darkness to another. I do not want my body to become totally dependent upon other people. I want my body to die while it can still hear a little, see a little, and most of all, when it can still think."

⌐ LESSON ⌐

Decisions our loved ones make are theirs to make, even when we don't understand and are hurt by their choices. It is our job as their advocate to support what they want from their life and to find a way to love them unconditionally.

You'll get a look at how to make ethical decisions for another person as you read the next chapter.

CHAPTER SIX

Making Decisions for Another Person

Substituted Judgment: A New Way of Thinking

I'll confess, this concept was difficult for me to grasp initially. My first thought in nursing had always been based on the patient's *best interest*. Step one: assess the situation. Step two: implement whatever would help the patient improve. Antibiotics for infection, surgical repair for a hip fracture, tests to clarify a complicated diagnosis. It was not until my company was asked to serve in the role of *Court Appointed Guardian* that I was exposed to the concept of *substituted judgment*.

The basic premise is to make decisions by looking not through your own eyes, but through the eyes of another person. To see not necessarily what is best medically, but what the other person would *desire*. Undeniably, this is formidable. The doctrine of substituted judgment asks a surrogate decision-maker to attempt to objectively determine, with as much accuracy as possible, what decision a now-incompetent patient would make in a particular situation if he or she were competent to do so. This involves examining the patient's morals, beliefs, and historical behavior patterns from the time he or she was competent.

If thinking for another seems daunting, it may help to look at your own intimate relationships. Many couples learn naturally and unconsciously how to practice substituted judgment as they communicate, negotiate, and live together day-by-day. Most couples can finish each other's sentences and order for each other at a restaurant; it simply comes from the years together.

This was useful to consider as I approached my new role as court-appointed guardian, requiring me to see through the eyes of the incapacitated person. It felt strange and unfamiliar at first, but has become instinctual at such a deep level that it is impossible to imagine otherwise. Think about it: If you were stripped of your decision-making capacity, would you want a surrogate to make choices based on their values or yours? In our nation, founded on individual rights, the appropriate and ethical approach seems clear.

When advocating for another, the principle of substituted judgment should be the first line of thinking. This is the founding principle of the *Age Your Way Program*. I believe each of us has the right to live life our way. None of us lacks an opinion, but many lack communication and documentation to ensure our wishes are followed.

> **⌐ EXERCISE ⌐**
>
> Do you feel strongly about decisions that may be made for you if incapacitated? If yes: List three things you'd like your advocate to know about you and your wishes. Make certain you communicate these wishes in writing.

Gary suffered a massive stroke at the age of sixty-three, leaving him unable to speak, walk, feed himself, or handle basic physical care. An unmarried loner, he'd left no clarity regarding his wishes and nobody in place to make his legal decisions. Without pre-planning, the medical system moved Gary through acute care and extended rehab for nine months. Although this is unusual, it sometimes happens. It was only when options needed to be considered regarding discharge from rehab that the void became apparent; incapacity with no legal decision-maker. Gary's improvement over the nine months had all been physical: walking, eating, and drinking. Sadly, he had not progressed in talking and reasoning. He was totally incapacitated, unable to return to independent living, could not name a responsible party, and needed court-appointed oversight. My company became his legal guardian.

The guardian role was to make choices for Gary as he would for himself if he could, following the doctrine of substituted judgment. But what did Gary see, what did he want? His words were no help, so observation of his behavior was the only guide. His violent temper tantrums clearly indicated what he did not want and observation gave me limited insight in to his pleasures: TV, coffee, and smoking *frequently.* In today's society of non-smoking facilities and non-smoking campuses, this was a challenge. But with special negotiation and signed waivers of liability, eventually we found a facility for Gary that allowed him the right to smoke at will. The temper tantrums subsided and Gary fell into a quiet routine. This was the best I could do under the circumstances, but the best never felt good enough.

⌐LESSON⌐

Start your plan early if you want control. Scrutinize your options to find the person you would trust most to make decisions through your eyes. Communicate your priorities and fears to help them get it right.

Tim was intellectually disabled from birth. To make matters worse, he went on to develop schizophrenia and bipolar disorder during his teens. He lived in facilities with care staff from the age of thirteen so his parents focused their planning on Tim's long-term financial needs. They did an excellent job in ensuring resources were available to provide him supported care for the remainder of his life. However, they fell short in making a comprehensive plan. They abdicated care decisions to the facilities where Tim lived.

Once, Tim ran away from his care facility in Texas all the way to Mexico. His childhood friend finally found him in a white stucco church, praying for help on a wooden pew beneath a statue of the Virgin of Guadalupe. Tim's friend convinced him to return, although life would not be easy, and care was complicated.

At the age of forty-five, Tim responded to the voices in his head telling him to jump from the second story at a shopping mall. No telling what the voices were saying, but the slow process of healing from fractures of his pelvis and both hips was almost more than Tim could stand. With the stress, the voices rose to a terrifying crescendo. Tim devised a strategy of hitting his head to make the voices go away. It didn't work, but it gave him something to do.

When Tim's parents died, his care decisions transitioned to the owner of the facility where Tim lived. At the time, this seemed to make sense. Since there was a financial trust in place, the fiscal piece was managed and the medical community accepted the facility owner's authority. Why not? This person had been a long-standing fixture in Tim's life. In time, however, questions arose about her legal right to make decisions as well as a potential conflict of interest. No checks and balances were in place. Were decisions being made in accordance with Tim's wishes or for the benefit of the facility owner? Third-party professional monitoring was initiated.

Obtaining dependable information was a challenge. Because of Tim's incapacity, data sources were limited to the facility owner and medical records. On the surface, everything appeared to be in order. However, Tim's inability to advocate for himself meant I needed additional time to complete a reliable investigation. Clearly, earlier decisions had benefitted the facility owner. Were these also choices for the benefit of Tim? Months passed as a concerning trend emerged.

When adequate evidence was compiled, the case was referred to probate court for determination, resulting in his lifelong friend being appointed as Tim's legal guardian.

This was the friend who knew how to find Tim in a remote church in Mexico. The appointed guardian had known Tim from childhood and dug way below the surface to ensure decisions were made in a manner that placed Tim as the priority. There was no conflict of interest as the newly named guardian was not in a position to benefit financially from any decisions made. Simple terminology was used to extract Tim's preferences, thus giving him a voice. He was warmed by the caring and he thrived. I've never seen such a positive and dramatic change in any one individual. The guardian clearly understood how to make choices on Tim's behalf, according to Tim's wishes.

On a crisp October day, I visited Tim at *his* home. Yes, living in his own home with caregivers dedicated to him. The house is single-story with a handicapped accessible shower to accommodate his physical disabilities now and into the future, being also wheelchair-accessible. With his recent diagnosis of diabetes and renal failure, meals are prepared to merge his preferences and dietary restrictions. During my visit, Tim was all excited, preparing for a trip to Tennessee. He had wanted to go for some time and now was the time. Tim, his caregiver, and his guardian would soon be on their way. His guardian is one of my heroes.

~ LESSON ~

Ethical decision-making by use of substituted judgment is the gold standard. Maximizing quality of life and self-determination is possible even when faced with catastrophic injury or disease. It takes caring and advocating for what that person would choose. What brings them pleasure and makes their life worth living must become your guide.

~ EXERCISE ~

At a restaurant with a partner, close friend, or a family member, play a guessing game about what the other wants to order. Did you get it right? Did they?

Extend the game beyond dinner choices to test your potential advocates' understanding of your thinking in other decision areas: personal, financial, medical. This is a valuable tool to train others specifically on who you are and how you think.

At times we need to make decisions for others that might cross the line of what we believe is acceptable. Read on about how drugs and alcohol might impact decisions and those we love.

CHAPTER SEVEN

Legal Substance Abuse

*The Art of Negotiating Choices
That Others Make*

Legal substance abuse is a controversial topic. It is also a significant problem in our society at large, which is reflected in my patient population. In the United States alone, more than fifteen million people abuse prescription drugs. Fifty-two million Americans over the age of twelve have used prescription drugs non-medically in their lifetime. The United States makes up five percent of the world's population and consumes seventy-five percent of the world's prescription drugs.

Since alcohol is legal and requires no prescription, it is readily available and perfectly acceptable in many environments. As of 2014, more than seventy percent of the population had consumed an alcoholic drink in the past year with twenty-five percent over the age of eighteen reporting either binge drinking or heavy drinking in the past month.

With prescriptions being doctor-written and alcohol legal for adults, how do health care providers negotiate the impact these substances have on our patients? I've found this becomes more of an art than a science. When these choices are made by individuals with capacity, then we have to accept what makes another person's life worth living as their choice. If there are opportunities to mitigate the negative effects, then we seize the opportunity.

The only patient I ever "fired" was a drug addict. Since the age of nineteen, Matt had been unable to control his body's movements because of a condition called dystonia. He said it felt like a leg cramp assaulting his whole body, jerking his muscles painfully and at times sending him crashing to the ground. As a result, Matt lived on a cocktail of muscle relaxers, narcotics, seizure inhibitors, and mood stabilizers. None of these were mild medications or low doses. The combination Matt was on by the time he was in his fifties was astounding. With the advent of pain management doctors, Matt was only able to obtain his medications by personally visiting the doctor each month. Of course, this was difficult because he was frequently too sedated to arrive at appointments on the right date and at the right time.

The only family member still associated with Matt was his out-of-state sister. All of his other relationships were burned by bad behavior, theft, and emotional drain. Matt's sister retained my company to assist in any way we could to keep Matt under medical care, on government benefits, and at a distance from all family. I learned about being caught in the web of manipulation and attachment, erecting barriers only to let them down again, and I learned about the grip of drug dependence.

Many times, I would wash and dress Matt in his bed, then half-drag him to his doctor appointment so we could obtain the needed prescriptions and avoid the pain of withdrawal. We worked together for nine years, with the exception of the year he disappeared on the streets and was unreachable, when he was officially *fired* from case management. However, when Matt reappeared in need, I took him back like the old friend he was.

As a result of the year on the streets, all Matt's health and government benefits had vanished and everything had to be re-established. As far as the government was concerned, with no identification and no residence, he simply didn't exist. I had no idea what an undertaking it would be just to obtain a legitimate photo ID. What a job! We worked together, jumping through every hoop until we finally achieved the impossible—a Texas ID card. I still consider this one of my greatest accomplishments.

Since drug abuse was an unfamiliar area of clinical practice for me, I had to look to Matt for instruction, even as I became the protector he called "Mama Bear." Group meetings were held with his drug-using friends who all signed agreements to not share used needles. I kept Matt's apartment stocked with sterile syringes and needle disposal boxes. We devised secret systems so his addicted "friends" wouldn't find and raid his stash of carefully hidden prescription narcotics. We moved from one doctor to another as Matt burned bridges, but we remained a united team. Drug dependence was such a part of Matt's life that my job was to keep the drugs flowing. If I failed, he would turn to the streets again with a greater risk of harm. We had success and we had failure. But mostly we had an honest understanding of what he needed to make his life worth living.

I'll never know for certain the condition surrounding Matt's death, but it was not foul play by an outsider. Behind the locked door of his apartment, his life ended with a self-induced overdose. To this day, I believe there was no intent to end his life; simply a case of a bit too much of "a good thing." According to Matt, his quality of life was the best it could be under the circumstances. He taught me how to abandon judgment and simply be his loyal advocate.

⁀ LESSON ⁀

When you become the support for another person, your function is to sustain what gives meaning to their life. If you can't fulfill this role with caring (which is difficult), then hand off the job to someone who can. Transferring responsibility can be a positive way of demonstrating concern.

Although legal, alcohol is a drug and every bit as addicting as habit-forming pharmaceuticals. Alcohol may even be more addicting, because it is so socially acceptable and readily available. At the start of my nursing career, I was horrified when hospice patients mixed alcohol with their morphine. I sought purity in health care and medication management. Over time, my patients taught me that long-standing alcohol dependence can create a need as real as that for oxygen. In countless cases, this must be respected, even if it is counterintuitive to a medical professional. Clinical management is tricky and medication dosages may need to be adjusted to accommodate for alcohol, but I found this to be another skill that can be learned.

I also learned that alcohol dependence can sometimes be more psychological than physical. In the end stages of life, when patients begin losing their balance and falling, we become adept at gradually decreasing wine and increasing cranberry juice in that lovely crystal wine goblet. Maintaining the same drinking routine provides the needed emotional satisfaction. To know which way to go with maintaining or decreasing alcohol requires a sincere evaluation of the individual patient, not a choice based on your personal value system. Rather, it must be about what gives the patient satisfaction and what he or she can tolerate. My best guide for this has been from direct patient caregivers. It is as much an art as a science; all a part of individualizing the patient's plan of care.

Next we'll look at a complex subject: family relationships. As touchy as relationships are throughout the years, illness and aging can make this an even greater challenge. The secret is to prepare, communicate, and adapt.

CHAPTER EIGHT

Family Relationships

Timing, Role Reversal, Consensus

Families are as unique as snowflakes. Not only is every person an individual, but each relates to other family members in their own unique manner. Changes in health status and aging can bring out the best and the worst in people. Every time I think I've seen it all, another distinctive scenario unfolds. Patients and families view needs differently and often the person in need resists care with the very last ounce of strength in their body.

WARREN: CHAMPION OF SELF-DETERMINATION

Oh, Warren, how I miss our many arguments! You were one of my greatest challenges.

When he was fifty-eight and at the top of his game, Warren rewarded himself with a surfing trip to Hawaii. But the game changed in an instant, from one wave to the next, when he lost control and the six-foot surfboard smashed into his spine. He washed up on the beach like driftwood, and would have died if not for a good citizen who started CPR. Drawing on his body's inherent will to survive, Warren embarked on a journey of anguish. Instincts propelled the care forward; treat what was treatable, sustain life at any cost. With a functioning brain, the body must be saved.

Quickly, the situation became overwhelming for his traveling partner, the girlfriend, who faded away in the night and was gone. Scared, alone, and still in Hawaii, Warren soldiered on. From the neck down, no movement, no sensation. What he did have was a ventilator to sustain breathing, unrelenting pain from spasms, a feeding tube for nutrition, pressure sores, a urinary catheter, and a will of iron. Each day felt like a thousand hours. The simple transition from lying flat to sitting upright took months to achieve. No part of his body functioned normally. Except his brain.

Because his two brothers and mother were in Texas, nearly four thousand miles away, Warren set his mind on returning to the Lone Star State. He knew there were milestones to reach first, which included getting weaned off the ventilator and taking food by mouth. Both were accomplished at a snail's pace. Patience—not in Warren's hard-driving nature—was mandatory. Drawing on personal connections at the highest level of health care, the plan for relocation commenced. Moods vacillated between anger and depression, sometimes on an hourly basis. Lashing out alternated with contrition. Every fiber of Warren's being cried out for control but there was none. Only his mind.

A renowned master chef, he knew how to run the show. In his professional career, he had command over every aspect—planning, directing, slicing, and dicing to achieve perfection. He could do it again. Same skills, different scenario, more on the line. Again, this called for patience beyond his capacity, and antidepressants to level out the outbursts. Would he ever leave Hawaii? He longed for family, but also knew himself. Family in the same town could cramp his style, diminish his independence, drive him crazy. Two hundred miles away was acceptable, so he was carefully loaded on an air ambulance plane, headed to Austin.

When I first met Warren, I knew he would demand the best I had to offer, and more. His brilliant mind and disabled body presented a stark contrast. His need to regulate everything was palpable. The requirement for a nurse to direct his complex medical care was overwhelmingly apparent. We debated, negotiated, talked hours on end. His treatment of caregivers was shocking to witness as he was both kind and cruel. With amazing tolerance, he would train his private care staff to perform medical procedures that were complex beyond any training they had. Then, he would turn around and blast the same caregiver with language to make a sailor blush. Caught between nurturing and attacking, the care staff was always on edge. Turnover was excessive.

Warren felt entitled to make unhealthy choices, and because of his mental clarity, he *was* entitled to do so. Missing doctor appointments made it hard to obtain needed prescriptions. Warren taught me how to beg, plead, and find new doctors. He also refused to be physically turned on a regular basis (to prevent pressure sores) and insisted on staying home alone at night. We both learned how to function in spite of sleepless nights of worry.

When all the talking in the world would not persuade Warren to make better choices, I turned to his family for reinforcement. Fine with him, they could join the fray and talk all they wanted, but he wouldn't allow them any influence, a common scenario. His brothers and mother lived within two hundred miles, eager to help, heartbroken over both the injury and Warren's poor decisions. They'd been an emotionally close and loving family, kept at a geographic distance from him for six years as Warren ruled his world.

While Warren, his own worst enemy, asserted his independence, he developed extensive pressure sores that almost ended his life. He survived as a result of multiple surgeries, a new colostomy, and three weeks in the intensive care unit. This was a moment of opportunity for a transition to a better situation, which could include family involvement as a constant in Warren's life. The family and I huddled up to craft the message: There was inadequate support in Austin, necessitating a move to where the family lived. After endless discussions with Warren and his agree-to-disagree attitude, the move was made. Hugs all around and promises to stay in touch. That was two years ago and he is doing well. I still get updates and think often of this man with the strong mind and injured body. I miss him.

⌒ LESSON ⌒

Timing is everything. A baseball bat swung too soon or too late will not connect. It's okay to delay executing your plan until the moment when it has the best probability of success. When that moment comes, move forward quickly and decisively.

CARL: REVERSAL OF LONG-STANDING ROLES

Carl was a determined individual. He taught us all many lessons, especially how to garner strength for the right cause. My first introduction to him was when his wife needed care. Her dementia was advanced and her daughter (Millie, Carl's stepdaughter) knew her mother's care was inadequate. Carl was an influential retired Washington D.C. attorney whose word had always been gospel. Nobody had ever doubted that he had the solution to every problem but, in the case of his wife's illness, he did not. To say the family meeting went badly is a gross understatement. His six-foot-three-inch stature and booming voice shut down any discussion of care. Millie cowered, consistent with their long-standing relationship.

Despite Carl's initial success in dismissing his wife's needs, it was hard for him to avoid the truth once repeated falls left her with a black eye and fractured wrist. But he held his ground until the day she wandered lost through the neighborhood to the busy street nearby, wearing only a nightgown. Police were called to return her home and concern escalated. Soiled clothing and a thirty-pound weight loss made this proud and beautiful Junior League leader unrecognizable, and she silently cried out for an advocate. Millie's need to safeguard her mother eventually surpassed her fear of Carl. The required strength didn't materialize overnight or without emotional pain and fear. Role reversal after a fifty-year relationship was gut wrenching.

Eventually, Millie took the essential steps to become her mother's court-appointed legal guardian. This transition of power was possible only if Carl was judged unfit. Millie trembled throughout the court hearing as mounting evidence was presented, but the decision was clear: Millie prevailed and became her mother's guardian. We feared family relations would be damaged beyond repair. Strangely, that was not the case, because Carl opted to ignore the day in court, as though it never happened. Care in the home was initiated and a *new normal* was established.

⁓ LESSON ⁓

Role reversal is painful but possible. Sometimes it's like standing on the top of a seventy-story building. If you're afraid of heights, look forward but never down. Strength grows when focus on the patient's needs is unyielding.

LESLIE: THE LAST BEST HOPE

Leslie was a mess throughout her life. Brought up by two alcoholic parents, her destiny was to follow in their footsteps. She was wracked by an anxiety disorder, alcoholism, and frequent falls. She had a hard time raising four children and holding on to her marriage because all family members bore emotional wounds. But life wasn't done with this clan. At fifty-three, Leslie was slammed by a stroke that took the tenuous family dynamic to a new level of dysfunction. Her husband adopted a lasting habit of giving in to whatever brought peace and the adult children were relieved just to be out of the house. Clearly, the new scenario called for a grounded decision-maker who could plan objectively, not emotionally. I was unsure whether any family member could fill the role.

We were able to move forward by having an exchange of candid communication with six people around the table: Leslie's husband, all four children, and myself. Old hurts were allowed to verbally flow, which was imperative to the family-meeting technique. The honesty was impressive, cathartic, and necessary. As a nurse, I was experienced with the path they would face in the years ahead so I asked questions and stayed quiet long enough to hear their answers, understanding that the likelihood for success would increase if they identified the solution themselves.

Who would be able to make decisions based on facts, not emotion or deep-seated hurt? What were their thoughts on care? Leslie's husband was the first to decline becoming her agent, as he had never been able to stand up to her demands. Three of the children dropped out one-by-one, all honest, all wounded. The last child standing was the daughter who lived a thousand miles away. She agreed to accept the mantle of legal decision-making, if my company would serve as the day-to-day clinical manager. The relief was palpable as everyone agreed.

I don't mean to present this case as easy, because it wasn't. There were numerous painful crossroads over the years. However, the clarity of a designated decision-maker allowed the family to move forward with order. Because the other four parties had "opted out," they were one-hundred-percent supportive of the daughter's decisions. She did an excellent job of sharing information with the others, diminishing surprises.

~ LESSONS ~

1. When a family meeting is called for, two things are critical: openness and a willingness to truly listen. Drop traditional roles and let everyone speak without judgment. A great deal is accomplished by simply allowing everyone to be heard. The gathering may require a mediator to maintain neutral ground rules. Credentialed mediators are available in most communities.

2. Just as in business, appointing a single decision-maker can be the most effective strategy. But with family sensitivities, consensus on that role helps ensure success. And going forward, the decision-maker needs to keep the family informed.

There is no magic pill to "fix" family relationships. Some are so fractured that repair is not possible. You probably know if that describes your family or not. From my point of view, with the patient clearly in my line of sight, what I seek is peace for the patient. When individuals are either elderly or injured, the last thing they need to negotiate is the family feud. Don't make the patient the rope in your tug of war. Some suggestions are:

- Refuse to disagree in front of the patient.

- Don't make the patient choose sides.

- When talking, use "I" statements. Communicate how *you* feel, not what others have done wrong. Others are more likely to hear what you say if you're not assessing blame.

- Stick to the subject at hand. No gunny-sacking of old hurts.

- Concede that you are willing to meet in the middle for the sake of agreement.

- Retain a mediator if needed to keep talks on track.

- If agreement cannot be reached, then your options include:

  - Power of Attorney or Guardian, which gives you or another the right and obligation to serve as the responsible party/agent to make decisions.

  - Having other family members interact with the patient at different times from the agent. Do not criticize the responsible party or discuss differing opinions. Focus on the patient and what brings them happiness.

  - It is always my hope that family relationships can mend with the right motivation. Recognize that the longest relationships you will have in life are with your siblings. Finding peace has the gift of longevity, providing long-standing closeness between brothers and sisters.

Even when family is one hundred percent aligned, there are other ways we can lose control as the following chapter demonstrates.

CHAPTER NINE

Other Ways We Lose Control

Let Me Count the Ways!

Even with advance planning, loss of control can happen by way of financial exploitation, missing medical clues, denial, failure to engage, and long-standing emotional damage.

FINANCIAL EXPLOITATION

Because this is such a burgeoning business for the unscrupulous, I'll briefly mention three different stories of financial wrongdoing. It's impossible for me to comprehend how anyone could steal from a vulnerable person, but there is more exploitation of the elderly with every passing year.

Jean hired the most economical home caregiver she could find because of limited finances. Her wish was to remain in her home, but this was only possible if she stretched her dollars. The worker she found was excellent with all care responsibilities; plus, she was astute at writing checks for her own weekly pay. The problem was the weekly paychecks were written *daily* and happily signed by Jean. Who would ever know? Jean managed her own finances with no oversight. It took more than a year for this reality to surface. By the time it was apparent, the goal of remaining home was no longer possible.

Even sadder is Sarah's story, because a family member was the culprit. Her son spent months of *selfless* devotion caring for his elderly mother. He lived with her, drove her car, and managed her medical care and all her expenses. He even quit his job to become her full-time paid caregiver. All her friends were so impressed with his loyalty. But when all resources were depleted, her son was gone, along with Sarah's life savings.

Then there's Maria, whose grandmother's engagement ring was stolen by one of her rotating caregivers. The heartbreak that followed was life-changing. Maria knew which caregiver was guilty, because the young lady moved out of state immediately after working her shift. Even though the police showed up and completed a full report, they couldn't afford the necessary manpower for an investigation and arrest. Without a conviction, the bonding surety company would not pay. The reality was that no amount of money would make up for what was irreplaceable. A tangible piece of Maria's history was gone along with her ability to trust.

All of these demonstrate true losses that were never resolved. Jean, Sarah, and Maria were all mistreated by people they knew and trusted. Such financial exploitation of the elderly is believed to be widely underreported for many obvious reasons. However, the estimate is in the billions.

⌐ LESSON ⌐

Devise a system of checks and balances, including some-one to monitor financial accounts. Either a trusted family member or service provider who is licensed and bonded can serve to oversee expenditures. With in-home care: Secure or remove checkbooks, credit cards, cash, and valuables (both financial and sentimental in nature).

MISSING MEDICAL CLUES

As we age, it's not uncommon to lose awareness of illness or injury, because pain sensitivity declines. The silver lining is that the elderly typically need less pain medication than the younger generation. In my hospital nurse experience, for example, it was common to see a fifty-year-old patient and an eighty-year-old in the same ward for the same hip replacement surgery. They experienced vastly different pain control requirements. The old and the oldest old can recover nicely with either minimal or no analgesia; a single Tylenol may do the trick. Maybe this is an attempt by the universe to be kind to the elderly. However, the positive aspect of this can be swiftly outweighed by the downside. Pain has a purpose: It serves as a valuable warning of a problem. It propels us to action. Without pain, both illness and injury often go untreated until too late. Treatment delay can lead to a more complicated medical situation.

Samantha always distrusted the medical community. Throughout her life, she was proud to say she needed a doctor only once a year to write her annual prescription for thyroid medication. Otherwise, she was the picture of health into her nineties. The day she called me to say she was too tired to get out of bed, I knew something was wrong. I found her short of breath, with a pulse rate of two hundred, and in the middle of a heart attack. She had no idea.

Arthur at eighty-eight was burly and proud, living on his own, managing his farm with no assistance from anyone. To say his surroundings were "untidy" would be putting it mildly. It had been more than 20 years since his wife died so he saw no reason to keep the place clean or do anything extra. It was the ultimate man's home, meeting all his needs. Out-of-state family saw him yearly for holidays and stayed in touch by phone. One day, his daughter, a teacher, heard a difference in his voice over the phone, but was unable to get time off from work to see for herself. She called me to go out and gather more information.

When I arrived, I was greeted by the smell of urine even before crossing the threshold to shake Arthur's hand. Two weeks prior he had fallen, hauled himself up, and continued his routine. Yes, he admitted to having some back pain, but that was nothing new to a farmer. Yes, one leg was dragging behind, but he expected that as part of natural aging. I saw a marked weakness of one leg but had no idea if this was a new or old situation. Arthur couldn't tell me either. Fortunately, he was a reasonable man who allowed me to take him in for x-rays. The leg weakness and urinary incontinence both were related to nerve compression from a newly herniated disc that could have caused permanent damage and even paralysis if untreated. Arthur had the required surgery immediately and recovered completely. Then, it was back to farming as usual.

⌐ LESSON ⌐

Pay close attention to even minor complaints from the elderly and observe for subtle changes. Be on high alert for changes in these areas: physical, mental, energy, appetite, weight loss, pain, falls. Early medical evaluation may avert disaster.

DENIAL (ALSO KNOWN AS PROCRASTINATION OR LYING TO OURSELVES)

Although some changes are too stark to be overlooked, most often we gradually adopt a new normal without acknowledging the subtle differences taking place. When our family member can no longer use the phone, we attribute this to failing eyesight or poor dexterity. When verbal responses come slowly or answers are inappropriate, this can seem like hearing loss. When we take over the grocery shopping or laundry for the sake of efficiency, we allow ourselves to move blindly past a cascade of decline. Deceiving ourselves allows us to hold on to the way things were and not implement protective changes.

Sally and Edward were practically joined at the hip. As a childless couple, they became everything to each other. They taught together at the university, traveled to exotic countries during summer breaks, remodeled their 1960s home with their own hands, and grew succulent foods in their garden. Their extended family was at a distance, visiting yearly for holidays. This allowed the couple's gradual decline to go unnoticed. But one Christmas, family members gathered at their house for lunch and noticed the food wasn't quite right. Help was needed. Sally and Edward both were thinner, and both were coughing. After lunch and presents, everyone kissed and hugged good-bye and went back to their busy lives. Six months later, Edward died of "sudden" lung cancer and Sally was lost to mid-level dementia. The family's denial was over. Sally was unable to shower independently, could not write a check, and was totally lost. It was only in looking back that their family was able to identify the changes that had been happening for some time. Denial had prevented them from seeing the truth as it unfolded.

⤳ EXERCISE ⤳

Document the things your elderly loved one can do independently. At the same time, note tasks that require help or are becoming difficult. Continue to update this list at intervals to identify trends and creeping inabilities. A written log works against denial.

FAILURE TO ENGAGE

I know, I know, we are all terribly busy—especially the sandwich generation, caught between dependent children and dependent parents. According to the Depew Research Center, one in three adults with a parent over sixty-five have financially contributed to parental support in the past year. The vast majority of this financial support (72 percent) is for ongoing need. With the drain of time, money, and emotion, there is an understandable aversion to dig deeper.

Unrelenting frustration is the best way to describe Lisa's story. She was a vibrant widow in her late sixties, still as beautiful and charming as ever. Her only family was a son who lived on the other side of the world in Italy. In his mind, his mother was still the independent woman he left behind fifteen years ago. He was busy with his life, struggling to keep his small business solvent, and grateful that his mother was not one of his problems. As far as he was concerned, she was doing well and needed nothing. The reality was quite the opposite. Lisa was confused, anxious, and unable to leave home on her own without getting lost. Neighbors became the support network keeping this lovely lady from harm. When I first met Lisa, I easily understood how her son could be misled. She chatted about her hectic morning—a workout at the gym followed by a meeting at the church. These *were* activities she truly remembered. However, they hadn't occurred that morning, but rather many months ago. Short-term memory impairment had confused old events for new ones. Neighbors had deliberately disabled the car and she had not left the house.

When I phoned Lisa's son to explain his mother's decline, I was initially cautious. These delicate communications need to be gentle but convincing. Often the family requires time to absorb the sad news. With each subsequent call to Lisa's son, I became less subtle, more brutally honest. No appropriate response ensued. He simply would not engage in the solution because no financial support was needed and direct communications with his mother were pleasant and problem-free. Over the next four months, he was bombarded by calls from neighbors, the doctor, the church, and from me. But he was too consumed with his own life and too far away to participate. As case manager, I assisted by taking Lisa to doctor appointments and setting up her medications. However, she was unsafe alone. I found a dementia facility that would provide her comfort, mental stimulation, and safety.

Since her son had Lisa's power of attorney, he needed to sign the facility's admission paperwork because Lisa was incapacitated. Still no action. I would lie awake nights hoping her son would schedule a visit or respond in time to avert a crisis. My communication to him escalated, bordering on harassment. To quiet me, he sent a friend to stay with Lisa and observe first-hand what was happening. That was all the verification needed. Her son then acted and Lisa transitioned to the dementia facility. Her personal belongings were moved in advance of her arrival at the facility and Lisa never commented on the move, never objected in any way. To this day, Lisa happily continues to function in the unofficial and self-appointed role of concierge at the facility, consistent with the lovely person she is.

⌐ LESSON ⌐

If you are not geographically close to family, stay in touch with their friends and neighbors to proactively monitor changes. People are slow to inject themselves into your life and the life of those you love. When others begin reporting problems, *listen!*

THE EMOTIONAL ROLLER-COASTER

Emotional injury is an adversary so great that it can permanently block progress toward planning. In contrast, aging can provide the opportunity for emotional healing. Personality traits either magnify or fade with age. Sometimes aging brings about changes that can allow a relationship to mend if you start soon enough.

I remember clearly the son of one of my most eccentric patients, a ninety-seven-year-old matriarch who refused to use a walker because walkers were for "old people." When younger, she had sternly ruled her domain and all her relationships with an iron fist. I found this harshness was part of her past, not her present. In aging, Elisabeth held some strong opinions but evolved to become a jovial lady, overflowing with laughter and joy. Traveling from England and full of dread, her only son dared to visit after a twelve-year hiatus. He was astounded to see how his mother now interacted with her world. He asked me, "What have you done with my mother? This is not the woman who raised me! If this had been my mother, I wouldn't still be on the psychiatrist's couch every week of my life."

In other cases, however, corrosive hurt and cruelty not only endures but grows with aging. Abusive relationships fester, leaving no room for kindness, caring, or healing. With the shift in power, grown children are in the position to exact revenge on the person who hurt them the most. Sometimes, old wounds reopen, but I've also seen families work hard, seize the opportunity to heal, and reconcile.

Valerie wrote the book on being a bad mother. She was spoiled and wild. Her only daughter, Beth, was raised by grandparents when Valerie went to prison for using and distributing heroin. After prison, Valerie tried to be a mother to Beth, but this only caused more damage to an already-wounded child. Valerie never even considered being a responsible mother, and would leave her young daughter alone and afraid. Beth quickly returned to the security of her loving grandparents' home.

In later years, when Valerie became incapacitated, Beth was the only family member available to help. But Valerie was no longer able to connect in a meaningful way, leaving no option for healing communication between mother and daughter. When Beth tried to assist, old scars opened and hemorrhaged. For self-protection, Beth opted for a court-appointed guardian to step in. That was the kindest act of love she could muster.

⌐ LESSON ⌐

Challenge yourself to mend fractured relationships while repair is still possible. Waiting too long may remove this as an option. A wise manager told me many years ago, "It's not the things you do in life you'll regret, but the things you don't do." In the sad instances when a relationship is beyond mending, accept that fact and work around it.

If you're feeling down, don't lose faith. Enjoy the next story of an amazing woman.

CHAPTER TEN

Long-Distance Caring

*The Story of Lois & Confessions of
What We Did Wrong*

Lois is the person I would most like to be—and whose temperament I would most like to have—if I had a choice. I marvel at Lois, my mother-in-law. Now in her nineties, she continues to demonstrate enviable traits: Acceptance, living in the moment, and just moving on. Growing up with five brothers and five sisters on a Kansas farm, family life was about cooperation. There was no complaining, merely acceptance of what they had. When the Great

The very remarkable Lois

Depression and Dust Bowl descended on Kansas in the 1930s, all possibility of their farm surviving dissolved. Moving on, the family packed up their car, single mattress tied on top, and headed west. Once in Oregon, Lois' father died, leaving the children to work while their mother ran the household. Lois and her siblings spent summers picking berries by day, sleeping in tents on the farm by night. These efforts paid rent on the house and allowed Lois to attend school in the fall.

How many of us take indoor running water as a basic entitlement? Not Lois, as she first experienced this luxury as a high school girl. Small luxuries, big appreciation, true acceptance of whatever life brings—that was Lois growing up, that is Lois to this day.

In her teens, Lois worked at the weather station, climbing a high stairway with no railings to take readings every hour. Nothing changed when she broke her leg; the stair climbing and hourly readings continued. During World War II, Lois volunteered for the Coast Guard where she met and married Gordon in 1945. A year later, she gave birth to the first of her two sons, Hank (my husband). Always a worker, Lois juggled marriage, two sons, and a career. With great accuracy, she mastered statistical typing for aeronautical firms. In 1960, when her boys were thirteen and eleven, a freak accident took Gordon's life, leaving Lois a single mother. I don't know where she drew the strength, but Lois raised two of the most remarkable men I know.

To stay positive, Lois surrounded herself with what made her happy, decorating her ceiling with rows of hanging colorful petticoats, like clouds in the sky. To stay active, Lois took up square dancing, wearing Western outfits propped up by her petticoats. Through dancing, she met and married her second husband, Ron. Together, they collected vacation days and traveled worldwide at every opportunity, making their life increasingly full with each passing year. Once again, sadness touched Lois when Ron died of cancer at the age of fifty-nine. Although Lois never remarried, she continued square dancing, exercising, traveling, and enjoyed the longest romantic relationship of her life, Otto.

Why share the story of Lois? It's because she taught me personally how difficult it is to care for elderly parents from afar. In spite of loving Lois dearly and working in the field of aging, we made mistakes, primarily because the distance between Texas and California colored our reality. On visits to California, we continued to view Lois as we always had: remarkable, independent, capable. But like Sally and Edward's family in Chapter Nine, we were guilty of denial.

The first indication of age-related changes came for us when Lois was in her eighties, when she answered a phone call. "Hi, it's your favorite grandson," the caller said. "Kevin, is that you?" Lois answered. The stranger on the phone said yes, he was grandson Kevin. Who else? He was in Europe and needed $2,500 wired to him immediately. Along with the money, he needed a promise from Lois to not mention this to his parents because he knew how this would upset us. The money was wired and the secret kept. Months later, when Lois asked us about Kevin's trip to Europe, the truth of the fraud emerged. We believed this to be an isolated incident and failed to dig deeper. *Financial exploitation* of Lois. *Denial* on our part.

> ### ～LESSON～
>
> At the first sign of financial concern, it's wise to perform a full inspection for irregularities. With a single incident, you're likely only seeing the tip of the iceberg. A huge and lucrative industry exists to exploit the elderly.

Our ultimate wake-up came in the form of a phone call. Lois was in ICU on life support. As a result of an untreated urinary tract infection, she had become septic and almost lost her life. This was a catastrophic change. For many years, Lois had always sensed when antibiotics were needed for her frequent infections. With age, Lois had regressed to the stage of *Missing Medical Clues*. Without family in town, there was no advocate and no monitor. We should have known better. Directly out of the ICU, we relocated Lois to Austin, our hometown. Typical of Lois, she accepted the situation and moved forward. No lingering goodbyes to people, no picking over precious items in her home. Acceptance, what an incredible and underrated trait. I marvel at her every day.

> ### ～PERSONAL LESSON～
>
> I'll never be Lois, but I can always strive for that as a goal.

For those of you who are determined to try long-distance caring in separate cities while your aging parents are still living at home, I hardly know where to start. It's exhausting both physically and mentally, plus it carries a dubious probability of success. As much as I hate to say that, it's simply the truth. On your own, it seems you can never get ahead of the curve, because every time you patch one hole, there is a new leak. As your loved one loses capacity, you assume responsibility for every conceivable task. You must either travel the distance to take care of everything yourself or arrange for services in the hope that they'll be done properly. All your efforts are compounded by both geographic separation and reluctance to accept help.

At a distance, how can you possibly monitor home deterioration, power outages, lawn care, doctor visits, medication management, safety, nutrition, hydration, personal hygiene, solicitation, exploitation, bill payments, even the mail? You can't. What you can do is wear yourself out completely and prove that you did everything possible before a change becomes absolutely necessary. Unless you're willing to contract a local case manager to be the responsible party, you're sunk. And while retaining a case manager to oversee everything is a good option, it is cost-prohibitive for the vast majority.

The danger of long-distance caring is that it provides a deceptive insulation, comforting at first, but based on a false innocence. What you don't know, can't hurt, the saying goes. Wrong. It's like simmering embers, simple to extinguish when small. Unattended, can be totally out of control. I have seen only two options that succeed in long-distance situations: Retaining a local responsible party for monitoring or relocating to live in the same city. My case management company is the local responsible party for many individuals who simply refused to move. Again, this is a viable solution, but also an expensive one. I have also seen countless patients successfully relocate to be near family. Although initially arduous, the benefit becomes apparent after the settling-in period. With physical or mental decline, it is more effective to go through the one-time pain of moving than to attempt remote management on your own. Once living in the same city, the reality of decline becomes crystal clear.

~ LESSON ~

Start planning relocation options for your distant family members well in advance of decline. The need can arise quickly, leaving little time for research. Sometimes the best facilities have waiting lists, so getting on the list can provide an added level of comfort. This planning can take place along with long-distance management. A great number of relocations occur at a time of crisis.

Everyone who is a parent or has a parent should read on about some of the most extraordinary parents in the world.

CHAPTER ELEVEN

Childhood Injuries & Intellectual Disability

The Most Extraordinary Parents in the World

Through the years, I have been endlessly amazed by the emotional fortitude of parents who raise their *children* for far longer than the expected number of years. Most of us watch with pride as our offspring reach milestones and gain independence. In life's natural evolution, we begin life helpless, evolve to being on our own, and then gradually revert toward dependence. But when your child is injured or disabled, then their dependency can last a lifetime. I use the word "childhood" in this chapter's title in a broad sense. Some children are disabled at birth or when they are young.

Others become ill or disabled in adulthood and return to their parent's loving arms for care. Whatever the path, I see parents who reach deep into their souls for a special brand of strength, both physical and emotional. I admire and honor them for every moment they spend, every task they perform. There is nothing easy about having to change diapers and physically lift your thirty-year-old child.

The reason this topic is included in the book is because disabled children become dependent adults, aging from the moment of their injury. This can happen to any one of us at any time. In these situations, there is little time to plan or evaluate, only the overwhelming demand to act. And the propulsion towards action goes on for years and years. These parents learn how to do more with less—less energy, fewer resources, less knowledge. They tackle and achieve what they never believed possible. They perform magic, day after day, year after year.

One of my patients is a young woman, Kylie, who contracted meningitis at eleven months old, resulting in catastrophic brain damage. She's never spoken a word, never had a purposeful movement of her limbs. Now in her thirties, she is happy, smiling, delighted in life. Why not? She lives in her own home with her mother lifting Kylie's ninety-pound body like a baby, feeding and diapering her, doting on her every need. The bond the two of them share is palpable from the moment you enter their lovely home. With the excellence of care provided, there are no medical complications, no problems. But the clock is ticking.

Kylie's father and adult sister are involved with her inter-mittently, so both understand her needs. However, neither of them could or would surrender their life to make Kylie the center of their world. This is a story of "only a mother's love." That story begins with selfless heroism. But the last chapter, which has yet to be written, has the potential to end in chaos, as I've discussed with Kylie's mom during our regular planning meetings. Kylie's sister has agreed to become guardian when their mother can no longer fulfill the role. I'm confident that can work. However, indecision continues over where Kylie will live next. Will she relocate to the city where her sister lives? When and where will she move to a care home or facility? These adjustments are so challenging that I've encouraged Kylie's mother to manage the transition while she is still able to handle her daily care. Although for her it would be a step to unknown territory, requiring cautious oversight and much trial-and-error, she's clearly the best choice. Mom knows Kylie better than anyone, has all the answers, knows all the tricks to try. However, Kylie's mom is reluctant to take the first steps, which is neither surprising nor unusual.

Cases like Kylie's often arrive at the steps of my company when parents delay too long, failing to plan for the future. Such delay is a natural result of too little time, too much fear, and a combination of blind love and denial. Nobody will ever be as devoted, as caring, as tireless as the natural parent—and nobody could ever understand a disabled child as well. However, someone must take over responsibility when the parent is gone. The only uncertainty is whether the transition will be planned and executed or if it will be a chaotic disaster. Yes, you may be irreplaceable, but even Broadway stars require an understudy—and your understudy can only be the most effective if you allow him or her the time to train, to absorb the gravity of the role, and to benefit from your guidance.

My case management company fulfills the role of court-appointed guardian for many individuals who spent their entire life in need of help, totally incapacitated. When this transition is necessary, it is a challenge as it often coincides with the death of a parent. In many of our cases, no foundation has been laid and many unanswered questions await us. In an ideal world, every disabled child would have a plan of how to live on without their parent. Items for the parent to plan would include the following:

- Establish a Special Needs Trust with funds to be utilized for personal expenses that are not paid by medical coverage or government benefits.

- Apply for and get all government benefits in place.

- Transition the child out of your home environment into a supported living environment, while you are still alive and able to supervise the new routine so that any issues can be resolved during your lifetime.

- Document your child's needs and idiosyncrasies. What makes them happy? What are their fears? What calms them?

- Leave a family history that includes contact and statistical data on parents, siblings, and others important to the child's welfare.

- Select the best fit to succeed you as guardian. Make the transition to the successor guardian while you can still actively train this person.

❧ Document health history and medical preferences for your child. *The Blueprint to Age Your Way* can serve as a guide to medical decision-making that you believe would be most appropriate.

❧ If possible, prepare your child for the eventual transition to the new responsible party. Introduce the successor guardian and involve them in your child's life.

⌒ **EXERCISE** ⌒

List what you've learned about your child — idiosyncrasies, habits, pet peeves — things that may not be readily apparent but would be important for a caregiver to know. Use this to begin your written transition plan. Initiate training your successor. Begin the search for future living options.

I am well aware that I address this area as an outsider. Only the parent of a disabled child can comprehend the texture of their child's life, the richness, the beauty, the depth. My thoughts arise mostly out of experience when the parent is suddenly no longer available to do their magic. I offer you my suggestions about transition with an overwhelming abundance of respect.

Now we'll consider a huge challenge we have as a nation: How to treat (or fail to treat) mental illness.

Mental Illness

A Challenge Worth Fighting

It seems to me that medical and psychiatric treatment are on two entirely different tracks. Medical treatment is moving forward each year with expanding facilities, more innovation, and greater success with symptom management. In contrast, I see options shrinking for my psychiatric patients. Although psychiatric medications continue to improve, the structure to ensure needed care has simply disappeared. Why? It's primarily money. Without adequate reimbursement for the cost of care, psychiatric facilities end up being closed down. Another factor has to do with admission regulations. Psychiatric patients can be admitted for inpatient care only voluntarily or under court order declaring them an imminent danger to themselves or others. Voluntary patients can leave any time they wish, so they often walk out when therapy hits a painful nerve or when they are past the crisis that brought them in. The burden of proof for danger can be so arduous that this option is often abandoned. Let me share a couple stories with you.

Louise, four-foot-eight-inches tall with her curly black hair and piercing blue eyes, looked like a little doll. But unlike a doll, she had a complicated existence. An inherited defect in her chromosomes was responsible for her small stature and compromised heart. But that was just the start. By the time I met Louise, she was 44 years old and living in a psychiatric group home. She had been cared for in various psychiatric homes since the age of seventeen. Medical conditions included diabetes, problems with thyroid regulation, and marked hearing loss. But her most constant ailment was schizoaffective disorder, bipolar type. With this condition, she suffered from hallucinations and erratic mood swings, depression then mania. When she was wildly manic and talking incessantly for weeks at a time, she was aware enough to discuss her symptoms, but still had no control, and couldn't stop talking. In a depressive cycle, Louise would regress to a near-catatonic state, almost impossible to arouse. The mood swings were the most extreme I ever witnessed. With her childlike appearance, all I ever wanted to do was to wrap her in my arms and protect her.

The challenges seemed endless. Her psychiatric condition improved only with the harshest of medications, so these were prescribed from the time she was a teen. However, her endocrine abnormalities (low thyroid and diabetes) impacted her ability to absorb the medication, resulting in a cycle of drug toxicity. Sweet as sugar, Louise tugged at everyone's heartstrings while she rode the roller coaster up and down. For a number of years, stability set in like a gift. The highs were lower and the lows were higher; relative calm.

This stable period ended at the age of 55, when the spiraling swings returned with a vengeance. Although inpatient psychiatric hospitalization was indicated, Louise's physical fragility meant she needed an acute medical hospital setting. There she would stay for weeks, mattress on the floor for her safety, either whirling like a banshee or in a near catatonic state. For about a year, she rode the see-saw, alternating lengthy hospitalizations with brief group home stays. Our preference for the long term would have been for Louise to live in her group home where she'd been most comfortable and where all her friends resided. But it was not to be. Eventually, a dementia home was the only facility that would agree to admit her for an extended period. The move was heartbreaking. Still looking like a child, Louise was a stark contrast to the other residents, who were frail and elderly with varying levels of dementia.

It took months for Louise to settle in to this very different environment. Time was needed to stabilize her medications and maintain that narrow range of therapeutic dose. But the care staff knew what to do, how to accept the rapid flow of words and how to coax her out of a deep slumber to provide nutrition. And they knew how to care for this *child* in their midst. A success.

I also had the opportunity to help another young lady with schizophrenia. Melanie was a beautiful, smart, talented, and well-educated woman whose symptoms began when she was in her twenties and caused her to mentally flounder for years. Her delusions caused her to hear voices, voices that became her friends, but fractured her family support network. In spite of a previous hysterectomy, Melanie imagined she had been raped and was pregnant. She gained more than 50 pounds as she planned to outfit the nursery for her baby. She also wrote letters to President Obama about his pending assassination, which earned her a personal visit from Homeland Security.

Melanie also denied that her mother was her "real mother," adding another layer of pain to the family. Her delightful mother did all she could and then sadly turned to the court system for help. I was appointed as guardian and vowed under oath to get Melanie the help she needed. But she didn't want help because that would mean letting go of her closest friends—the voices that had accompanied her for years. My first face-to-face encounter with Melanie required three policemen. One officer was at the front door, one at the back, and one outside Melanie's bedroom. After the police safely extracted Melanie from her bedroom, we assembled at the dining room for our first painful conversation: Melanie, her mother, the police, and me. With inherently good manners, Melanie firmly rejected care and involvement from this court-ordered outsider. The painful memory of that day remains clear and uncomfortable in my mind.

Our relationship was strained to say the least. We went to psychiatric appointments but Melanie refused her schizophrenia medication so we made no progress. Three months after we began working together, I intercepted a letter Melanie had written to the FBI in which she made outrageous accusations and requested a gun. Propelled by fear for Melanie's safety, I began my first-hand experience in surmounting one barrier after another in an attempt to obtain the needed inpatient psychiatric help. It took twelve gripping hours, three separate police departments, two mental health deputies, and a paramedic to finally get Melanie transported to a psychiatric facility.

On arrival, Melanie informed the attending psychiatrist that she would decline care, so the psychiatrist refused to admit her for an evaluation. It made no difference that she was delusional and that I was legally authorized to request the evaluation on her behalf. Due to Melanie's rejection, they were prepared to do nothing. We'd reached a stalemate: As the country-western song goes, you've got to know when to hold 'em, know when to fold 'em. Out of frustration, I left Melanie in the admissions department with a promise of litigation against the hospital if any harm came to her while on their premises. Only then, with me gone, did they take her in for a comprehensive evaluation. However, the facility gave her no medications because of Melanie's continued refusal. There she stayed for weeks, hallucinating and untreated, while I took a stab at fighting the system.

Following three weeks as an inpatient, salvation for Melanie came through my appeal to a wise and caring judge who presided over the mental health court. With an abundance of tenderness and respect, he explained to Melanie that medication was the only way her disease of schizophrenia could be treated and then he ordered the facility to administer the medication. Once medicated and stable, Melanie returned home with a regime of therapeutic monthly injections to treat her disease. Within months, the voices disappeared and Melanie's disease was under control. Within a year, her guardianship ended as it was no longer necessary. Four years later, she continues her healthy life with restored family relationships, a job, independence, and happiness. The judge will always be one of my heroes. Melanie will always be one of my stars.

An epilogue to the story of Melanie is what happened a few months after her recovery and return to the "real world." Living with her mother, Melanie thwarted a medical disaster in the making. Her mother experienced a rapid physical change, but couldn't name what was happening. Melanie evaluated the situation, and took action before the aneurysm in her mother's heart burst. She literally saved her mother's life, making this a remarkable outcome and so much more. Two of the finest women I have ever known were saved.

Sadly, this type of success is rare. All patients have the right to refuse care or to discontinue medications. I applaud the commitment to personal freedom behind this approach, but in practice, it fails many individuals who can be helped. What can be done? Support. Yes, support funding at all levels—city, county, state, federal—for mental health and indigent care. The vast majority of people with untreated mental health issues are indigent, so their solution comes from greater options for care, both through outpatient and hospital solutions. As a society, we also need to support long-term compliance with psychiatric medications; not only support, but applaud loudly.

⌐ EXERCISE ⌐

Write your congressional representative in support of enhancing meaningful indigent and psychiatric care. Follow the news and write again after high-profile psychiatric events happen.

Caregivers—you walk the lonely road of the everyday champion. I salute you. The next chapter is in your honor. Enjoy.

CHAPTER THIRTEEN

Caregivers

You Make the Difference

Caregivers, I love you dearly because you are the change-makers. In your capable hands, what was horrible can become wonderful. This is true whether you're an employed aide or a family caregiver serving as the responsible party. Family, you stretch yourself into a net beneath your loved one, catching every stray concern, ensuring every possible step is taken to mitigate decline, advocate, and ensure security and comfort.

These family saints may not be donning gloves and changing diapers, but they are vital caregivers, indispensable. What I see so often is that a family caregiver travels a lonely path. A swarm of others may come and go, unloading an abundance of advice. But a single person usually bears the ultimate burden. This is the one who falls asleep at night and wakes in the morning worrying, the person who can't leave town without a huge lump in their throat, the one who jumps every time the phone rings. Eventually, their form of caregiving may evolve to obsession, because they are flying solo without ever having a day off. For them, the mantle of responsibility is not removable.

If you're that special person, I bow to you. It has been a gift to work with so many remarkable family caregivers over the years. Of course, this chapter can't be written without sharing some stories to help convey warnings and lessons. The first family caregiver story I'll tell involves my husband, Hank, who struggled to fulfill this role for his aunt. Hank has always been the most solid, calm, grounded person I know. He never gets ruffled or upset. It is simply not in his DNA. Remember, his mother is Lois (my remarkable mother-in-law). His dear aunt lived in California. When her husband died, she was left with no family nearby and she needed assistance. We arranged for her to relocate to our city, Austin, so we could provide her with ongoing love and support locally. We knew Sisty's memory was failing but, until she moved near us, we had no idea about the changes in her personality and judgment. Oh my, what a shock. Nothing we could do was adequate, in her opinion. And I mean nothing. The towels we bought her weren't acceptable because they weren't her towels, so we transported the threadbare ones from her old home. She told us her gorgeous view of the famous Texas Hill Country was terrible; where were the stores? She complained that the food was causing diarrhea and the people in the assisted-living facility were so old that they tottered around on walkers. Misery all around.

But she was great at using the phone. She called us as often as six times per hour. Every day, she demanded Phillips Milk of Magnesia and kept calling every ten minutes until the bottle was delivered. She consumed a whole bottle of laxatives every day but wouldn't budge when we tried to tell her that was why she had diarrhea. No dice, it was the food. She berated us constantly: She was miserable and it was Hank's fault. For the first and only time in our long marriage, I saw Hank suffer the highs and lows of the family caregiver. More lows than highs, always trying but failing to make things right. He vacillated between logical understanding and checking flights to send her back to California *alone*. Our marriage was reduced to talking Hank off the ledge, trying to help him understand the attacks were not personal and were not about him. They were about Sisty and her dementia.

Within eight months, her medical and mental conditions worsened. She fell and fractured her femur, had a surgical repair, and fell again, this time fracturing her pelvis. Her dementia was so severe that it blocked her ability to participate in rehabilitation, thus halting any functional recovery. She permanently took to her bed. This dear aunt wound up needing the full support of a nursing home and hospice care. But sometimes, there's a silver lining. At this new stage, Sisty ended every visit with "I love you" as she was comforted by her family caregiver, Hank. The next four years of affection and meaningful attachment lasted much longer than the difficult times. Her last words before dying were "I love you."

⌐ LESSON ⌐

If you're the responsible party/family caregiver, there's no place to hide. It's all on you. Therefore, the best strategy for managing this marathon is to take care of yourself. Look for options: Counseling, getting away, taking real time out, anything that breaks the daily routine and brings you pleasure. It may not always be apparent, but you are a blessing and cannot be replaced.

The big difference between paid and family caregivers is that paid staff usually don't shoulder all the responsibility alone. At the end of the day, aides can retreat to their own home, even put up their feet. And if the going gets really tough, they can get out. Unlike family, an employee can quit. When the paid worker is struggling, family members should assume the patient is also struggling with the relationship. However, often the patient is less able to voice concerns. It's important that the connection between the patient and the caregiver remain therapeutic. If it's not, you can always look elsewhere for a replacement. But too many times I have seen families hold on to an ineffective caregiver just because the pain of changing is too great. Understandable. However, the right fit can change a patient's life from bad to good.

One patient I remember vividly with a challenging caregiver situation was Sam. He had no family, so he appointed his financial advisor as his legal advocate/POA (power of attorney). With an inoperable brain tumor, Sam was steadily losing control over bodily functions. Meanwhile, his ability to communicate eroded to the point where he could no longer report problems. The POA hired a live-in caregiver and retained me for oversight. At first, the care seemed fine. Sam was happy, the caregiver was focused. In my supervisory role, I made *unannounced* visits to the home (always the best practice). Before long, I saw lapses in care. Sam was hungry and in soiled clothing on one of my visits, nothing dangerous but certainly unacceptable. When confronted, the caregiver offered logical explanations. I put him on notice, informed the POA of my concerns, and made more frequent supervisory visits.

Within the next month, care improved and then fell off again. I discovered the caregiver was entertaining his friends at the patient's home. It was a tricky case as this was both the patient's home and the worker's residence as a live-in caregiver. Some leeway for tolerance was reasonable. The tipping point occurred when I arrived one day (again unannounced) to find the home filled with boxes of new tennis shoes and a swarm of strangers lined up to purchase the *bargains*. Sam was also hungry and dirty, crying in his bed. I cleaned him, fed him, and called a halt to the home-based tennis shoe business, insisting that the customers leave.

Of course, I contacted the POA to initiate an immediate change in care staff. The POA resisted. He knew the caregiver had no home of his own and had other pressing obligations. This horrified me as it appeared the POA was worried more about the live-in caregiver than the patient. I wondered why, and then realized it was because the caregiver could effectively verbalize all his needs and concerns. Sam could not.

I was convinced a face-to-face conversation would give me a better chance to influence the decision in favor of the patient. It did not. My next strategy was to threaten to report the situation to Adult Protective Services, naming both the caregiver and POA as negligent. That got results. We brought a new caregiver to the home with no notice to the current one. We all met outside the house in the dark—the new live-in aide, POA, and myself. Even then, it took an hour of debate to move the plan forward. The POA started to renege on his agreement because he still didn't want to turn his back on the current caregiver who had such dire personal needs. Once again I threatened to involve Adult Protective Services and finally the POA relented. It was terribly uncomfortable as we severed the current caregiver's employment and helped him remove his personal items from the home. When his belongings would not fit in his car, we waited outside in the cold with his pile of debris until his friends came to help. This was not the only time I've seen caregiver needs take precedence over patient needs.

Although this is a vivid example of a decision-maker subjugating patient concerns to other factors, I have seen subtle variations of this happen repeatedly. Self-serving care staff can be quite astute at involving family in their troubles, playing on sympathies. I have seen families purchase cars for the caregiver so they can report to work on time. True, there's an inherent dependence on paid helpers that is natural. They are difficult to find and maintaining the status-quo takes less effort than implementing changes. I get it. But what about the vulnerable patient? Shouldn't that always be the focus? Of course.

Although Sam's story was harsh, it is the exception. The
tenderness and heart of the good caregivers outweigh the
bad tenfold. People who touch you, feed you, wash you,
help you walk—they are the difference-makers. Most
caregivers I have the pleasure to work with know more
about the patient than the closest family member could
ever know. Over time, their heart beats in unison with the
patient. They know when things are stable and they know
when something's wrong, even if they can't pinpoint the
exact problem. All I need is a call from a *good* caregiver to
tell me, "Sadie looks different today," and I'm on my way.
Their antenna is more accurate than the most sophisticated
scanner. They simply know. Magnificent.

With a compassionate heart and a focus on making a
difference, miracles can happen. Consider Dottie, as stubborn as any woman I've ever met. At five foot seven and
two hundred pounds, she radiated power, and anyone who
argued with her did so at their own peril. You knew she
meant it when she said she intended to remain in her home
and manage her life under her own power until her last
breath. Then Dottie fell, and fell again. When the falling
continued, her family and doctor's message was clear: Such

falls were *not* a normal part of getting older, and Dottie needed help. But she dug in her heels. She pointed out she'd thrived on her own as a widow for many years, independent and self-sufficient, and she expected to keep it that way. So there'd be no help in the house, thank you very much.

Then came the day she crashed through her oversized glass coffee table. Following a mild head injury and a major set of sutures, Dottie was deemed incapacitated, which left her brother in charge. Poor guy.

At that point, I was called in to do an assessment and planning. There the fight began. Dottie was offended and humiliated that her brother was now her POA and decision maker. She hated my presence as the *experienced* outsider. She hated the official declaration that would allow her to remain in her home only if an attendant were present 24 hours a day, seven days a week. Dottie was furious, not about the expense but because it meant relinquishing power. She made it clear: if we brought in help, she would make their life a living hell. We did not doubt her word.

Caregiver selection was critical. In our interviews, we honed in on two primary qualifications: empathy and sensitivity. After hiring, we proceeded with baby steps. Staff stayed largely out of sight at first, coming and going through the back door of a downstairs apartment so shift changes wouldn't alarm Dottie. Her round-the-clock care was divided among three kind and gentle women. They all deferred to Dottie. In her home, she was boss, they were a variety of names.

At first, Dottie called them her *jailers*. They toiled largely in the shadows, purchasing and preparing food, washing clothes, tidying up when Dottie was in another room. Most of the time, Dottie did not even know they were present, although clearly she was clean and fed. When she did notice them, she spewed out a foul tirade of insults. The caregivers' strategy was to lock the safety gate at the top of the stairway, disappear downstairs, and wait for the storm to settle through the blessed magic of short-term memory loss. Meanwhile, Dottie's brother and I fortified the caregivers with respect, encouragement, and gratitude.

It took about a year, but a new normal took hold. The "jailers" became the "renters." In her cloud of her dementia, Dottie believed these unobtrusive women were renting her downstairs apartment. She allowed them upstairs for brief periods of time while Dottie assumed the role of landlord. Initial seeds of a relationship sprouted. The fact that there were three different women never seemed to register in Dottie's mind.

Their relationship entered its final stage when a cardiac problem sent Dottie to the hospital. Her "renters" followed, and stayed by her side. Now they were "my girls." When they transported Dottie home a week later, her girls became her security, her comfort, her constant companions. They loved her and she loved them; together until the end.

⌐ LESSON ⌐

The right caregiver is a precious gift, though the dependent patient may not see it that way initially (or ever). If the patient is stable and content, it's likely the caregiver's doing. Their job can be grueling, but should never be thankless. Praise them highly, and praise them often. It only takes a moment to express heartfelt appreciation with an abundance of gratitude.

Next we'll look at putting on your "bossy pants" and being the ultimate support person.

The Art of Advocating

Here's Your Official Permission

Like a delicious dessert, I've saved writing this chapter for the end. Although it won't appear last in the finished book, I've written it last as my own personal treat. I'm going to enjoy admitting to my brazen behavior, thus providing you official permission to be brazen too.

Advocating is how we make the difference for those we love. Standing big and being heard is not related to size or age or status. It's directly correlated to how much we care. Although I have never reached a hundred pounds in my life (pregnancy aside), I learned to go nose-to-nose with anyone when advocating for a patient, regardless of my opponent's size or position. In a hospital, a courtroom, family meeting, or a doctor's office, it's my job to speak for the patient in a manner that is heard. You may need to do the same for yourself or your loved one. Together, let's look at designing a badge of courage that fits and feels right for you.

Through the years, I've seen the big, strong, and powerful shrink when facing a situation they didn't understand. The secret is that you don't *have* to fully understand the rules and regulations, which are often just some bureaucracy's list of all the reasons that you can't get what you want. Go with your gut. Speak up when something isn't clear, doesn't make sense, or might hurt the one you are trying to protect. You may or may not be successful every time but the effort will gradually give life to your inner warrior, to call upon whenever you need to advocate for someone or something. And the times you are successful will make the fight worthwhile.

Late one Wednesday, the evening before Thanksgiving, a trust officer called me, pleading. Could I meet her at the hospital? One of her favorite clients had just received the surprise news that it was time to go home, and discharge papers were almost ready. The patient had no plan for tomorrow, or the next day, or the day after that.

Matt was smart and strong. After being held as a prisoner of war in World War II, he'd dusted himself off to earn graduate degrees and embarked on a noteworthy engineering career. However, a stroke and the subsequent recovery process left him so vulnerable and deflated he never thought of objecting to the ill-advised discharge. It took all his energy to figure out how to move with half his body paralyzed. Returning home without a plan would not only be foolish, it might be disastrous. But a plan takes time, and the hospital wasn't offering time.

I arrived, met the patient, reviewed his chart, and confirmed that discharge would be premature. Marching up to the nurse's station, black briefcase in hand, I pled Matt's case. At first they balked, but then I offered up the magic words, "unsafe discharge." It worked. Hospitals are legally and ethically prohibited from making unsafe discharges. The hospital administration caved. Matt breathed a sigh of relief, and the trust officer and I quietly agreed to serve ourselves an extra helping of gratitude that Thanksgiving. Matt remained hospitalized through the holiday weekend while I arranged care and equipment in the home to ensure his safety. We became the best of friends.

It helps to recognize the financial implications of various patient-care scenarios, keeping in mind that a hospital is a business, concerned not only with treatment and recovery, but also with profit and loss. Typically, hospitals receive standard fees for inpatient stays based on the patient's diagnosis. If the patient stays three days or three weeks under a single diagnosis, the hospital's payment is the same. So, of course, the hospital directs staff to discharge as quickly as possible. That is the burden of their position, the directive of their employer.

When conditions call for transitioning a patient to a skilled nursing facility at time of discharge, the nursing home selection criteria is like musical chairs: The patient goes via medical transport to the first nursing facility with an empty bed. It could be the best or the worst facility in town, but it's where the patient lands once the bed availability is confirmed—but not my patients. I slow down the process to make the selection based on verified quality of care delivered. That is the right of every patient and the role of every advocate. You can do the same.

If things are moving too quickly, too slowly, or just don't make sense, speak up. I've watched doctors enter a hospital room and announce to the patient that their IV (intravenous) fluids were being stopped so they could go home. I recall when this happened to one of my patients who'd been up all night vomiting, she was unable to keep down a single sip of water. Without an advocate, she would have gone home just to return within hours by ambulance due to dehydration. Even (and especially) if you are unsure what your loved one's symptoms may mean, you can and should communicate the facts. Speak for a patient who is ill or unable to speak for themselves. Information is the power you hold.

⌐ LESSON ⌐

Advocating doesn't take special training or knowledge. It takes caring, common sense, communication, perseverance, and the nerve to step on the brakes when hasty decisions are made. Your expertise grows from experience and learning from mistakes. Remember: Success is often built on a pile of failures. When you fail, you then know better what doesn't work. Celebrate your learning curve and be kind to yourself.

Not long ago, I met with Joe and Susie, a couple who were motivated to map out their plan for aging. Their number one priority was to remain together; number two was to stay in their own home. When all was documented, with their permission, I emailed their written plan and priorities to their out-of-state children. One enthusiastic daughter, Elaine, called me right away to inquire about facilities for her parents, completely ignoring their wishes to remain together and in their home. She was ready to act, with a scheme to move her parents to two separate facilities—assisted living for Joe, a dementia unit for Susie.

For a moment, I was speechless. Did she not receive the documents? Did she not read her parent's highest priorities? Yes, she did. But she was convinced her parents were caught up in vague nostalgia, a pipe dream. To Elaine, the written plan signified nothing. I assured her it was much more than a *passing fancy*; it was their *unambiguous* intent for their life. Signed, sealed, delivered. As Joe and Susie's advocate, I set up a phone conference with all the children, we clarified matters with a good talk, and the couple remained in their home together.

Joe and Susie's experience is just one example of what can happen with aging. Often throughout society, the elderly become sadly invisible. As their power dwindles along with physical or mental decline, many older people find it more difficult to speak loudly, to be heard. That doesn't mean their voice is irrelevant. It means that advocates have a job to do.

Joining your loved one at medical appointments is an ideal opportunity for advocating. To make the most of your few minutes with the doctor, do your homework: Create a clear, concise health and medication record so instead of racking your brain during the appointment, you'll have plenty of time to focus on issues at hand. Think through those issues, questions, and concerns in advance, and write them down. If the doctor wants to start or stop medications, ask enough questions to make sure you're comfortable with his or her rationale. If tests are ordered, are they really needed? Give yourself permission to probe, inquire, challenge.

One smart patient with whom I've worked for sixteen years taught me a profound lesson: *Only test what you will treat*. At the start of our working relationship, I was pushing for her to have a routine mammogram and colonoscopy. She assured me that regardless of the outcome, she would not treat for any findings. Her choice, point made, lesson learned.

Advocating in the face of poor care is a delicate balance, like walking a tightrope. This is true particularly for long-term support in a facility or at home. Of course, you want the best care possible for your loved one. You monitor the situation and observe what's right and what's wrong. Some problems are simple math: Expecting too much work in too few hours. Other times, substandard work may be traced to an unmotivated worker. Emotions run rampant. I've been tempted to shake someone by the shoulders and demand improvement. But I doubt that would work. Likely it would backfire with worse care to retaliate for my unkindness.

Over the years I've worked with numerous families to improve care. Sometimes an advocate can make a difference, other times not. The truth is, a stable staff is the best strategy. If every day brings a new caregiver, quality plummets. It takes time to understand the patient: What they like, what brings them joy, what causes pain. So take it upon yourself to advocate for staff stabilization. Talk with the management regarding assignments and turnover. When turnover has been constant and there is no expectation for resolution, then you may need to consider a move.

Some families place cameras in the patient's room to observe care being delivered. With staff "on alert," this may encourage better treatment, but it also could embitter workers already at the low end of the pay and prestige spectrum. Also, I worry a little about patient privacy as I think how I would dislike this option for myself. Before you go this route, remember to stop and ask the patient's permission.

When there is relative staff stability, put on your best sales hat and get busy building relationships with the care workers, especially the "hands-on" employees. Those are the people who make the difference. Once you can call them by name, work on catching them doing something right. Acknowledge the positive acts and express gratitude. Report their good deeds to management. You may be the only one doing so. When you determine who is involved on a daily basis, you can move to step two, getting staff better acquainted with your loved one. Offer bits of information, one piece at a time, at a rate they'll understand and retain while attending to a busy workday. Has your family member always had dry, itchy skin? Do they prefer their water with ice? Can they only sit up only for one hour before becoming fatigued? When you see aides adjust care based on the new information, be generous with thanks and praise. Their roster may amount to twelve patients that day so, if they personalize care for your family, take time to acknowledge it. Occasionally you may go even further, bringing little goodies to show your appreciation. But what's most important is simply recognizing a job well done. The work is hard and the thanks are few.

Serving as an advocate can be one of the most rewarding roles you will ever fill. It's not easy, of course. At times you'll scream in the closet simply to defuse frustration. That's okay. What isn't okay is screaming at others, as this moves you from advocating to fighting. Fighting is trying to hurt someone. Advocating is the act of supporting. Remember your objectives, continue gaining experience, and watch the positive results evolve.

Although you are advocating for another, you may be surprised by what happens to you in the process. Tremendous satisfaction can come from advocating in a difficult situation. Success can bring a life-altering sense of personal power and self-respect, qualities that will serve you well long after you've forgotten the challenges you faced on behalf of your loved one.

⌐ LESSON ⌐

An effective advocate must observe, plan, communicate, and step into uncomfortable situations for the sake of another. To take on the role is to invite failure as well as success, but if you persevere, the rewards may astound you.

Effective advocating in a facility setting requires:

- ✢ Staff stability
- ✢ A positive relationship with the staff
- ✢ Connecting your loved one to the staff
- ✢ Recognizing and thanking the staff

Before closing out this chapter, I have to share a cautionary tale about connecting the dots among various healthcare professionals. As Ada and her daughter Betty learned, a medically complex patient can get lost in the medical whirlwind, as one clinician after another tosses out sometimes conflicting opinions. With no coordination of care, doctors, nurses, and therapists proffer advice based on generalized medical experience, as though one size fits all and as though they are the only one offering advice. There is no thought about how all these *directives* impact the patient's quality of life. A watchful advocate should be able to forestall a debacle, but Ada fell through the cracks.

Ada suffered a stroke at the age of sixty, leaving her cognitively impaired and partially paralyzed. Within the year, her husband died. Their oldest daughter, Busy Betty, took on both legal responsibility and daily management for Ada, whose condition was complex. Ada joined Betty's household full of children, pets, and a job outside the house — a life already overflowing.

Betty escorted Ada to the multitude of doctor appointments to treat her various ailments, including brain injury, dementia, diabetes, depression, and functional disabilities. Each professional prescribed medications and advice to keep Ada healthy: Thirty minutes of exercise daily, no more than two cups of coffee a day, no beer, diabetic diet, no upsetting TV programs, eight to ten hours of sleep at night. Compliant Betty followed every recommendation to the letter so that by the time the last instruction was implemented, she became Sergeant Betty. Ada was forced into a life designed to maintain health at all costs. But it cost Ada's happiness. Not until the woman literally cried out in misery did anyone step back to consider the restrictions as a whole. Despite good intentions, she'd been forced piecemeal into a life not worth living.

What a disservice from those of us in health care. Never once had anyone paid sufficient attention or offered "food for thought" beyond what was medically indicated. The health system hadn't attempted an integrated approach or a broad discussion of options, how to possibly soften the effects, weighing pros and cons. Each clinician added another layer of restriction in their field of expertise, never considering how many other restrictions were already in place. Shame on us in the medical community, myself included.

> ⌐ LESSON ⌐
>
> Medical practitioners treat in their area of expertise; providing advice for the general population. The most astute patient advocate will function as a screener, filtering through the swarm of advice and accepting or rejecting what makes sense for the patient.

Next, the legal chapter, designed to make certain you have the essential documents in place for you and those you love. No lawyer jokes, this is serious business.

CHAPTER FIFTEEN

Legal Pitfalls

*Let's Look at What You **CAN** Control*

It always strikes me odd that most people have a will in place long before any other legal documents. The will concerns what takes place after death. But what about all the years while you're still alive? Those are the years in which your plan will be felt and experienced by you. Maintaining control while alive is what this book addresses.

If you do nothing else in planning, take the deep dive into your legal paperwork! Some of you will want to close this book right now at the prospect of such a dive. But wait! With guidance and grit, you too can swim. You can tiptoe into the water by checking online where you'll find some of the necessary documents, but read the fine print. States have varying requirements, so make sure the documents you download comply with your state's particular laws. Even better, meet with an attorney and execute all your documents as a group. Over the years, I have seen disasters averted by well-written and customized legal documents. True, an attorney costs money. But it's an investment, and you—and those who'll survive you or support you in the case of disability—are worth it.

You may think you're too young to worry about this. So thought Scott, who was injured in a bicycle crash when he was 23 years old. Before the accident, he lived in a world of possibility. But as soon as his head hit the concrete, the long years of "after" began. He could no longer talk, walk, or take care of himself. Emergency workers did their jobs and saved Scott's life. Of course they did: Scott was young and vital, and lacking documentation to the contrary, he was entitled to "extraordinary measures."

Nine years later, Scott remains in the same mental and physical condition, needing total care for the rest of his life. Court procedures were required to designate a guardian for legal authority to act on Scott's behalf, since he had no ability to consent or refuse treatment. Scott's mother became his court appointed voice. She also became the sponsor of all that is good and protective in his daily existence. I marvel at her tenderness and her strength, a perfect advocate. One can only guess at his quality of life, but the emotional and financial cost is astronomical. This situation could happen to anyone. Don't delay.

Four documents rise to the top of my priority list to help you in aging your way: Financial and Medical Powers of Attorney, Directive to Physician, and HIPAA Release. Only these will be explored in this book because of the impact they can have on your living years. You may notice that a will is not on my short list. I'm not saying a will is nonessential; after all, it does a great deal to diminish family pain and tumult after death. However, a will that takes effect after you die doesn't impact your quality of life, comfort, or choices while alive. I don't know what happens to us after death but I have experienced the heartache of patients with no voice being swept along helplessly inside the medical system while alive.

FINANCIAL AND MEDICAL POWERS OF ATTORNEY (POA)

Power of Attorney documents name the person you appoint to manage your medical and/or financial decisions or both should you become incapacitated. I will refer to this person as your *agent*.

In considering the ideal medical agent, ask yourself who you can trust to carry out *your* wishes if you can't speak for yourself. That's their job. In case your personal wishes differ from theirs, now or in the future, it's imperative to be clear in advance. Your wishes are the bottom line. Your agent must possess sufficient emotional maturity to stand firm against others who might want to exert their influence on decisions. Surprisingly, the ideal agent isn't necessarily the smartest or oldest person. Whom can you trust with your life? Listen to your intuition as you identify a surrogate whose moral compass is aligned with your own, someone level-headed and strong enough to stand up for you above all else.

When you've singled out this individual, you've only just begun. You also need Plan B, a backup agent in case your first choice doesn't work out. Especially if your agent is close to your age, you will need at least one alternate of a younger generation in case your primary agent dies or loses capacity before you do. Far too often, a named agent's death or incapacity renders legal documents ineffective. Without younger alternates, you may find yourself redoing documents, or even worse, your documents may become "stale" at a time where you no longer have the mental capacity to execute new ones.

So you've identified your agent and alternates. Then what? Now it's time to roll up your sleeves and talk frankly. Don't ignore your deepest fears, but listen to them and let them guide you. In no uncertain terms, tell your agent (and alternates) about what medical care you want and don't want. *The Blueprint to Age Your Way* outlines multiple scenarios to guide and document your discussion. I developed it after personally participating in hundreds of such conversations with families over the years.

Lucille's full life had been everything she could have wished for and more. She was ready to relax and allow her 96 years of living to take the natural course; no medications, no hospitals, nothing but comfort and love. Lucille gathered her family, clearly articulated her medical wishes and watched in shock as her family withdrew in horror. Only one person understood and accepted Lucille's wishes: 20-year-old Emma. No memories of the early years colored Emma's perception of Lucille, the spunky great-grandmother who'd seemed old from the day Emma was born. As the rest of the loving family objected, Lucille decided. The great-granddaughter was named the agent under Lucille's Medical Power of Attorney. Now Lucille could relax and enjoy the rest of her life, which amounted to two additional years in a "medical intervention-free" environment, exactly as she had wished. The additional years gave the other family members time to understand and accept her choices. The appropriate agent gave Lucille peace.

Like Lucille, you'll find a sense of relief when you elect a medical agent. Now, what about your finances? The best agent to manage your finances may be someone completely different from your medical agent. Failure to name a financial agent could leave bills unpaid and your life in shambles. Carefully consider whom you trust with financial management. If you have substantial assets (typically $1 million or more), you might consider appointing a corporate fiduciary, such as a bank, to manage your assets, rather than depending on a friend or family member to avoid any conflict of interest. A professional financial manager is employed by a company that can make you financially whole in the event of mismanagement.

To equip your financial agent properly, compile information in advance and tell your agent where these files are located. While you don't need to reveal the value of your estate, you should assemble items such as bank accounts, assets, obligations, and passwords. Think about it, could you step in and manage another person's financial life with no information?

⁓ EXERCISE ⁓

Write it down: Who will speak for you if the unthinkable happens and you can't make your own medical and financial decisions. Then write down two alternates, at least one from a younger generation. Ask if they are willing. Then meet with your attorney to execute documents RIGHT AWAY.

DIRECTIVE TO PHYSICIANS (LIVING WILL)

This legal document specifies *what* medical care you want if you develop an incurable or terminal condition. Your agent will employ it if you can't speak for yourself.

To crystalize the importance of discussing and documenting specific wishes, I'll tell you about Ruby. Brilliant and funny, she sparkled with energy until the age of 90 when she suffered a devastating stroke. Suddenly, she could no longer swallow or speak. This was a true heartbreak for Felicia, the devoted daughter who'd brought Ruby to live in her home three years before. They shared a special bond of heartfelt communication that should have made this sad event bearable. They finished each other's sentences. Ruby's stroke only strengthened their bond that now needed no words, and Felicia held Ruby's hand, thinking, "Whatever comes, Mom, I'll be here." Ruby had named Felicia as her agent and had executed a Directive to Physician emphatically ruling out artificial life support in the event of an irreversible condition. With a heart-tugging commitment to Ruby's expressed desire, Felicia was now prepared to ensure her mother's physical comfort and allow nature to take its course. Through Felicia's tears, her mother's wish remained crystal clear.

Then Ruby's other adult children showed up. Though they'd never before been involved in caring for her, they injected themselves in opposition, raising such a scene that the hospital's ethics committee had to devote hours to the family feud. Ruby's uninvolved children won. They forced the hospital to insert a feeding tube, because Ruby had never *specifically* detailed her thoughts about artificial feedings. In the end, the feeding tube provided no additional life, only additional sorrow. My heart still aches for Felicia, the daughter who was so good, so supportive, so connected to every beat of her mother's heart.

⌐ LESSON ⌐

If you don't direct your medical care, someone else will. Do it while you can. Document specific medical scenarios to avoid ambiguity, protect yourself and your agent, and avert significant heartache.

NOT A LEGAL DOCUMENT: OUT OF HOSPITAL DO NOT RESUSCITATE (DNR)

Few people get it. If an ambulance shows up at your door, do you think your carefully worded legal documents will protect your end-of-life wishes? Ninety percent of my patients and families think so. But they're wrong.

Your "Directive to Physician" is a valuable legal document, helpful in making thoughtful decisions with all facts considered. But its value flies out the window once EMS (emergency medical systems) is involved. For these situations, you need a different form, the DNR (do not resuscitate) document. This directs EMS to *not* perform CPR, if that is your wish, allowing a natural death instead.

In an emergency, EMS will never stop to read legal documents. When a patient has no heartbeat and isn't breathing, every second counts. Paramedics go straight to CPR (cardiopulmonary resuscitation). That's their job. They'll stop for just one thing: If someone hands them the out-of-hospital DNR form upon arrival to the house. Whatever your legal documents say about your living will makes no difference to EMS.

Therefore, if you or your loved one wishes to *allow a natural death*, you must complete the EMS document that clarifies this wish. Search the internet for the Out of Hospital DNR in your specific state. After you fill out the form, get your physician to sign it and keep it handy. With this completed form, EMS will continue to attend to all your emergent needs, transport you to the hospital when indicated, and manage other medical conditions. What they will *not* do is perform CPR after you have died. There will be no attempt to reestablish your breathing or heartbeat after they have stopped.

It's important to note, this document is specifically designed to be effective when *out of the hospital setting*. This can be in the home, nursing home, assisted living, or anywhere apart from the hospital. Once you enter the hospital doors, the Out of Hospital DNR form is no longer effective. However, your advocate may find it useful as evidence to argue your wishes, should you become nonverbal or incapacitated while in the hospital. The more extensive, specific, and accessible your advance documentation, the greater the chance your wishes will prevail.

If you can speak for yourself when admitted to the hospital, you can and should direct your "code status." In hospital lingo, "coding" refers to the moment when a patient experiences cardiac or respiratory arrest. "Code status" is the hospital's own term. Unless clarified otherwise, everyone is a "full code" when entering the hospital, which means CPR will be performed. Should this not be

your wish or not be the wish of your loved one, a talk with
the attending doctor will be needed to initiate a DNR order.

Know the difference between the EMS Out of Hospital DNR
form and your legal documents concerning end-of-life
wishes. The only document EMS can honor when respond-
ing to a 911 call is the EMS form, and the paramedics need
to have that form presented to them the moment they step
inside the home. In addition, understand that all patients
enter the hospital as a "full code" (CPR will be initiated)
unless the doctor writes an order to the contrary.

HEALTH INSURANCE PORTABILITY AND ACCOUNTABILITY ACT (HIPAA).

Your health records are private, protected by law. Unless
you plan otherwise, this protection can block your designated agent from getting adequate information to advocate
for you. Your legal documents should include a HIPAA
form permitting your healthcare providers to release medical records and communication to your dedicated agent.
Surprisingly, the rules apply even to a spouse; no HIPAA
release, nothing shared. Sometimes, a patient's simple verbal consent will open the doors to communication. Other
times, both the HIPAA and Medical POA documents are
needed. List the same primary agent and alternates on both
your HIPAA release and your Medical POA document.

To complicate matters further, some providers insist
their own medical release forms be signed before they'll

provide information. Imagine the problems this can cause if you're the agent for someone who can no longer communicate or sign an agreement. A well-meaning focus on patient protection actually can inhibit medical care and decision-making. When caught in this scenario, it helps to remember it's not personal, it's the policy of the facility. Take a slow deep breath and remember what you learned in the last chapter on advocating. Put on your bossy pants. Then ask for a supervisor.

Don't run away, you've come so far. In spite of the twists and turns, we need to look at cost and insurance coverage to evaluate options.

~ CHAPTER SIXTEEN ~

The Cost of Aging

Where Insurance & Government Benefits Can Help

Plans with and without money take different paths. For a very few people, money is no object. But for the rest of us, even those with substantial bank accounts, finances are a source of anxiety, especially in times of crisis. This chapter will expose you to ways you can find help.

Organization and planning can make the difference between feeling safe and feeling out of control. Feeling out of control directly impacts your health, because it increases stress and shifts your attention from physical well-being to money, at a time when health cries out to be the priority. When you need calm and clarity the most, you may face a perilous learning curve in order to access medical benefits and navigate other health-related financial concerns.

One thing you can do right away to gain control is to implement a routine of keeping pristine spending records. These files don't just take up space, they can save you money in the future. For example, to receive certain government health benefits, you'll have to show proof of need, sometimes with records going back as far as five years. (One reason is to make sure you didn't give away money to family in an attempt to qualify for indigent medical benefits.) Besides verifying eligibility for needs-based benefits, accurate records can enable significant tax deductions. Here's some motivation for you to keep track of spending:

1. The Medicaid program may try to interpret any financial help you give to a family member as a "transfer" making you ineligible for Medicaid for a period of time. If you can prove you later had expenses the person helped you with, that amount may be deductible from the amount "transferred." This is possible only if you can prove the amounts were "returned" by paying expenses. An elder-law attorney experienced with Medicaid regulations can guide you through this labyrinth.

2. Long-term care expenses (including the entire cost of nursing home, assisted living, or home care) may be deductible from your income tax as medical expenses. This can reduce your tax to zero—if you can document the expense. An attorney or accountant can help.

3. An excellent aid to planning your financial future is to estimate your future income and expenses. But without records to work from, nearly everyone underestimates expenses, which can undermine the whole plan.

~ LESSON ~

From the moment health care support is needed or anticipated (even in the planning stages), keep copies of every expense, every disbursement. Accurate records will help your financial plan and may save you money.

The combination of costly care and long life can brew a perfect storm of financial calamity. The stories you'll read in this chapter could easily be yours or mine: What we assume to be sufficient resources can quickly evaporate as situations transform. But knowledge is power. One of the best ways to protect ourselves is with a thorough understanding of health insurance and government benefit programs. Read on and learn.

Madeline was diagnosed with multiple sclerosis at the age of 23. Her disease was progressive, worsening over time. Within 15 years, she required a hydraulic sling apparatus to lift her from bed to chair, moved about in a motorized wheelchair, and needed help for all her activities of daily living (bathing, dressing, and all the things that able-bodied people take for granted). Unrelenting pain and profound depression added to the physical challenges. Madeline's husband began traveling more for work, while their teenage son absorbed the bulk of required duties. For him, enjoyable activities such as sports and friends became a distant memory. Employer health insurance covered medical costs, but all the other expenses required payment from out-of-pocket funds.

Emotional well-being dwindled along with the bank balance. The couple consulted an elder-law attorney to restructure their finances and help Madeline seek Medicaid custodial (non-medical) care. As part of the process, she had to live in a nursing home for months to establish medical eligibility. It was a nightmare for Madeline as each day felt like a year. Once qualified medically and financially, she eventually returned home with a Medicaid-reimbursed helper, authorized to spend eight hours per day delivering care. Finally, Madeline could stay in her own home with the people she loved and her familiar routines. Finally, her son could get back to being just another teenager on the basketball court. Finally, the bank balance inched into the black.

Criteria for indigent care benefits differ state-by-state. They don't make it easy: Sometimes the only way to manage the complicated application process is by consulting a paid professional. An attorney specializing in benefit programs is ideally positioned to provide you the state-specific advice. And now the broken record: Your well-documented financial records are the basis for qualification, along with medical qualification.

Skilled planning and records management also helps as you seek reimbursement from insurance plans in all their varied forms, whether Medicare, Medicaid, Obamacare, Tricare VA health insurance, private-pay or an employer program. Each has its own quirks, so I'll review them here.

Medicare is *health insurance* for individuals over sixty-five who have worked and paid into the system. During our working years, we watch Medicare dollars float out of our paychecks with an assumption that this will cover our later care. It does: Acute medical care, not long-term care. It also provides health insurance to younger people with disabilities, end-stage renal disease, and amyotrophic lateral sclerosis (Lou Gehrig's disease). It is a federally funded health insurance program with multiple options and varying costs.

Medicare Supplement plans and prescription drug plans are available for an additional fee once you've qualified for traditional Medicare. In addition, Medicare recipients can enroll in a *Managed Medicare* plan that covers both acute medical expenses and prescriptions. These plans can add a measure of control to monthly outgo, but carry some drawback as does any other managed plan or HMO: A restricted network of providers for care. Careful research is needed to make the decision that is right for you.

The Affordable Care Act (Obamacare) is a federal *health insurance* program enacted to improve the quality and affordability of health insurance and eliminate the pre-existing exclusion.

The Veterans Administration (VA) provides *health insurance* for those who served in active military service and separated under any condition other than dishonorable. Minimum duty requirements vary for the health insurance plan so anyone who served should investigate individual eligibility.

Tricare is *health insurance* for retired military members. It is government-provided healthcare with varying options. Once you reach the retirement age of 65, you can convert to "Tricare for Life" and enjoy double coverage with Medicare. Besides medical coverage, Tricare offers an excellent prescription drug plan.

Employee or private health insurance covers acute medical needs, just like those listed above. Some employers will offer options for long-term care insurance, which will be discussed below.

Medicaid is a *social health care program* for individuals with low income and limited resources. It is a means-tested plan, jointly funded by state and federal governments, but managed by each state. States differ as to who qualifies and what is covered. Medicaid recipients must be US citizens or legal permanent residents. Poverty alone does not necessarily qualify someone for Medicaid. Other conditions apply.

The scope of this chapter is not to answer specific questions about plan coverage. Instead, the purpose is to familiarize you with the types of medical insurance and to clarify the difference between acute medical and long-term care. All the above cover medical care as they are health insurance plans (Medicare, Medicaid, Affordable Care Act, VA, Tricare, and private health insurance). Each has an in-depth website and you'll need time to comprehend the complexities. But your time is well spent to read and understand.

One thing to keep in mind is that it takes patience to explore all the options. When signing up by phone, I've spent as much as four hours on a single call, left repeatedly on hold. My frustration was exceeded only by my fear that the phone line would go dead before I achieved my goal. If you're doing this for someone else, be sure you have every conceivable piece of information at hand when making the call (full legal name, Social Security number, date of birth, Medicare number, phone number, mailing address, mother's maiden name, amount of Social Security payments, and more). Food and drink by your side helps to survive the call.

For planning, it's useful to know basic terminology, and to understand the difference between acute and long-term care:

1. **Acute medical care** typically is delivered by health-care professionals for an episode of illness, usually taking place in a hospital, emergency room, or other short-term facility. Some outpatient diagnostic services also fall under this category.

2. **Long-term care** covers a variety of services for both medical and non-medical needs. These apply when someone has a chronic illness or disability and cannot care for themselves for long periods of time. This can address the six activities of daily living (ADLs) such as bathing, dressing, eating, continence, toileting, and transferring. Practitioners address the patient's chronic conditions. Care can be provided in the home, assisted living, dementia facilities, or in nursing homes. Long-term care can be further divided into three categories.

    a. Custodial long-term care: This non-medical care can sometimes, but not always, be covered by Medicaid or long-term-care insurance.

    b. Nursing home care: When defined requirements are met, this is covered by Medicaid or long-term care insurance.

    c. Skilled care: Usually covered by Medicare, Medicaid, insurance, and long-term care insurance if qualifying criteria are met. Limits as to length of coverage usually apply.

The goal of health insurance is to address acute medical care needs until *skilled care is no longer medically beneficial.* Then health insurance stops paying for care: skilled care has reached a point of diminishing returns and the patient has reached "maximum level of wellness," a euphemism meaning the patient will not improve because of the skilled care that is being delivered. They may improve naturally over time, but skilled intervention is no longer helpful. That's the point when challenges can become overwhelming.

You may ask, what about the months and years of care to manage long-term and chronic conditions after maximum wellness is attained? Who pays to manage the activities of daily living that are not medical but will continue forever? I'll share the current options that exist at the time of writing this book. This caveat is mentioned because plan coverages do change. However, you need some general rules to follow. Here they are.

Depending on the state and eligibility criteria, Medicaid may pay for purely custodial care in a nursing facility. They may even cover the cost of limited assistance in the home, as was the case with Madeline. Some VA programs do the same, either in a nursing facility or in the patient's home. However, VA eligibility depends on military-service history and financial requirements. The qualification process takes time and expertise. Apart from these two, you'll need to plan on long-term care insurance (LTC) or out-of-pocket payment to cover what is often the longest stretch—years of custodial service.

Long-term care insurance has been a blessing to many. You can purchase policies privately before you have health issues or if you have a well-funded employer—usually a large company—that offers this as part of their benefit package. It makes sense to consider the LTC insurance option. What's tricky is that LTC insurance can be costly. You may be tempted to "time" the purchase by waiting until you're older and more likely to need it—but once you start accumulating medical diagnoses, you may not be able to obtain coverage. According to the American Association of Long-Term Care Insurance, less than ten percent of those younger than 50 are turned down for coverage, compared to nearly 25 percent in their sixties, and 45 percent in their seventies. As you read through the rest of the book, I hope you'll keep LTC insurance somewhere in your mind. Countless patients are being helped to a better level of care because insurance is paying a significant percentage of the cost. At the very least, explore this as an investment to consider.

If you're one of the very few for whom money is no object, you'll discover that paying from your own pocket opens all options for supporting your loved one. Even so, it's wise to keep an eye on both assets and income. Monthly costs range widely from $200 to $20,000 per month, depending on how many hours per day the patient needs help. It's ideal to pay the cost of care from income alone and reserve assets for times of crisis. If you're regularly invading principal, you need a medical/financial assessment to confirm that total assets are adequate to cover life expectancy. Repeat this from time to time.

I recall Julie, a blue-eyed beauty, who had more than enough resources to remain in her own home with privately paid caregivers. She and her husband had worked hard and saved religiously. No financial worries, or so we thought—until Julie started showing signs that she

might outlive her savings. We changed her care at home
from hourly-paid staff to live-in providers to decrease the
cost. One caregiver worked four days, the other three days
each week. Julie was transitioned to a hospital bed with
side-rails and an alarm clipped to her nightgown. When
she attempted to get out of bed during the night, the alarm
would wake the caregiver who slept in the bed next to her.
This strategy helped stretch her dollars, but it only went so
far. Julie ran out of money.

Her devoted son sat in front of me and sobbed at the
thought of moving his sophisticated mother to a gov-
ernment-funded Medicaid nursing home. His pain was
palpable. With no other option, we made the move with
trepidation and awaited her negative response. It never
came. She did well, never changing her emotional balance.
The continued devotion of her son was ever-present, which
was all she needed to feel happy and loved. Julie lived
out the rest of her days in this stable and well-supported
environment. However, the same facility had many lonely
residents who were not so lucky. They had run out of money
and did not have the family support Julie enjoyed, or they
hated institutional life and would never have moved there
if insurance would have paid for home care. Each situation
is individual, some happy, some sad. Every scenario can be
helped by loving kindness, connection, and planning.

If you're concerned about finances being inadequate,
the essential person to help with planning is an elder-law
attorney who understands Medicaid and VA regulations.
Attorneys sometimes manage the "transfer penalty" with
planning that sets aside some cash or other assets that
would otherwise be used up before impoverishment leads

to Medicaid eligibility. More often, they help you *avoid* making penalized transfers that may leave you unexpectedly ineligible for Medicaid for months or years after all your money is gone. In general, a well-prepared attorney can help you get control of your own future by planning for the best care you can afford. In many cases this means *avoiding* Medicaid eligibility and getting better care using other resources. You cannot navigate this road alone. Contact an elder-law attorney in your community for help with planning for long-term care in the context of all your needs and commitments.

Add to this twisted road, the challenge when no financial information is available. Hundreds of families have come to me in a medical crisis without a clue about financial resources. That's why communication and documentation are both imperative: The sooner the better. At the end of the book, I'll expose you to a method to document information in one place for review, *The Blueprint to Age Your Way*. Don't allow yourself or your family to become a casualty of poor planning. The price is too high.

⌐ LESSON ⌐

Consider all options for payment of care: Medicare, Medicaid, VA, Tricare, employee/private health insurance, Obamacare, long-term care insurance, private pay. In making plans, keep in mind the difference between acute medical care and long-term care.

Now that you have a working knowledge of cost and coverage options, let's dig into the alternatives of where to live.

CHAPTER SEVENTEEN

Placement Alternatives

Where to Go?

In some countries, there's no question about where you'll go when you age. You move in with family, a cultural expression of honor, and remain in the family home for the duration. As we know, however, that's not the practice here. Many in the US feel trapped in the sandwich generation, looking after aging relatives, still actively involved with children and grandchildren, and working. During the day, our house stands empty, so if an older relative moved in they'd be alone and unsafe. Often, aging family lives far away, making daily support impossible.

I receive calls every week from families searching for *any* decent, safe place where Grandma might live and thrive. In the very best of circumstances, *where* to go is still a challenging decision. Innocent, ignorant mistakes are rampant. That's the reason for this chapter; to lend a helping hand, to explain various options, what they provide and what they don't. Keep in mind, moving is traumatic: Even more so if the place you choose turns out to be a blunder. That's why I urge you to begin your process when time is on your side, and to delve into careful research before action. With that in mind, the explanations in this chapter are presented to help you make better decisions. With a large volume of material, this chapter contains information instead of stories. If you are a coffee drinker, you may want to add a shot of expresso for this chapter. Are you ready?

The fact is that the vast majority of us want to remain in our home forever. Another fact: The vast majority can't afford it. As care needs increase, so does the cost—both financially and in terms of human resources. Hiring an in-home helper may make financial sense when needs are small: Assistance with groceries, bathing, housekeeping. But what starts small grows over time, while costs increase exponentially. Care at home is the most expensive option because you are paying someone to provide one-on-one attention. In a facility, by contrast, a single caregiver assists multiple patients, therefore reducing expense.

Let's look at the alternatives. The following grids compare nine primary options available today. In general, the lists flow progressively according to patient status, from independent at first to finally incapacitated and totally dependent. Patients' needs are not static: What seems appropriate today may be completely off-base a year from now. Many people transition from one level of care to the next over time, while some enter a facility needing a higher level of care and never move again.

Whether you're formulating your own long-term plan or you're helping Grandma in the short term, these are your options for care. Study and evaluate them, considering both the present and the future. Once you decide what would work best for you, communicate your wishes to the person you've designated as your agent, and to loved ones you trust.

1. LIVING INDEPENDENTLY IN THE HOME

When appropriate	Mentally sharp, able to manage personal care, safe from exploitation.
Financial cost	Typical home maintenance costs.
Payment sources	Private pay for typical home costs.
Human resources (family / agent)	May need someone to check status or be available for emergencies.
Personal care	Self-manage all Activities of Daily Living (ADLs) such as bathing, dressing, continence, eating, toileting, and transferring from bed to chair.
Safety (physical and financial)	Able to phone for help or push button on a wearable emergency alert if at risk of falls. Aware of solicitation and scamming. Will not provide personal identifying information or purchase non-legitimate services.
Medications	Take independently. Someone else may need to set up medications into daily pill compartments.
Medical care	Independently go to appointments, have someone else take, or have home-visiting doctor.
Nutrition	Maintain own meals. Drink adequate fluids. Can prepare simple meals. Meals on Wheels or other home-delivered food can be arranged.
Transportation	Can safely drive or can utilize other means of transport for groceries and errands.
Add-on services done by others	Housekeeping. Lawn. Anything else needed for the home. Emergency alert system for falls or emergencies.
Medicare-provided services	Intermittent Medicare visits at no cost after episode of illness, with doctor's order establishing need for some form of skilled service, and if patient is home-bound (nursing, therapy, bath aide). Hospice visits for end-of-life care.

Special considerations	Home must be free of fall risks, any stairs safely manageable, bathroom with grab-bars and other safety measures in place.
Clues it's no longer working	Patient is no longer clean, wearing the same clothes every day, losing weight, inadequate food in the home, house dirty, falls, exploitation.

2. LIVING AT HOME WITH CARE ASSISTANCE

When appropriate	When the home can be made physically safe and caregivers are able to provide whatever help patient needs.
Financial cost	Varies per geographic area. Can typically start at a few hundred dollars a week when care needs are small and intermittent. Dramatically higher cost when 24-hour care required; can be as high as $20,000 a month in some parts of the country. If patient sleeps well at night, a live-in caregiver can be used who also sleeps at night and is paid a flat daily rate. This can reduce cost by a third.
Payment sources for caregivers	Private pay. Long-term care insurance. Medicaid for low income (in some states & some circumstances). VA pension and/or "extended care services" for some veterans and their widow(er)s.
Human resources (family / agent)	Most patients need someone to oversee care. Family or third party to ensure no exploitation by caregivers (sad but true) or external parties.
Personal care	Any or all ADLs (bathing, dressing, continence, eating, toileting, transferring from bed to chair) can be managed by caregiver.
Safety (physical and financial)	Able to phone for help or push button on a wearable emergency alert if alone for periods of time. Home must be free of fall risks, any stairs safely manageable, bathroom with grab bars and other safety measures in place. Aware of solicitation and scamming. Will not provide personal identifying information or purchase non-legitimate services. Checkbooks, credit cards, and valuables made safe or removed from the home.
Medications	Can be independent or with caregiver assistance.

Medical care	Independently go to appointments, have someone else take, or have home-visiting doctor. Family or caregiver should be able/willing to drive to appointments as need arises.
Nutrition	Meals on Wheels or other home-delivered foods can continue. Caregiver can grocery shop and prepare meals.
Transportation	Search for caregiver who can grocery shop and take on errands / outings.
Add-on services done by others	Housekeeping. Lawn. Emergency alert system.
Medicare-paid services	Intermittent Medicare visits at no cost after episode of illness, with doctor's order, establishing need for some form of skilled service, and if patient is home-bound (nursing, therapy, bath aide). Hospice visits for end-of-life care.
Special considerations	Third party will need to oversee caregivers and monitor finances. Watch that patient is not incrementally paying for caregiver expenses as dependence grows and patient becomes involved in the caregiver's personal saga. Monitoring checking account(s) and credit card(s) online with patient's permission may be advisable.
Clues it's no longer working	Depleting financial resources. Resisting caregiver services. Denying or refusing need for care. Personally unclean. Losing weight. Falls. Exploitation.

3. LIVING AT FAMILY MEMBER'S HOME

When appropriate	When the home can be made physically safe and family is willing to be "on call" 24 hours a day, seven days a week. In most situations, should be for a limited time only.
Financial cost	May have renovation costs to make house appropriate /safe for an elderly or handicapped individual. If family is working, caregiver cost may be a part of the financial formula; cost varies with hours of care needed.
Payment sources for caregivers	Private pay. Long-term care insurance. Medicaid for low income (in some states & some circumstances). VA pension and/or "extended care services" for some veterans and their widow(er)s.
Human resources (family / agent)	Human cost is huge as the household changes dramatically. Family should have a written agreement in advance to include expectations and what would constitute a need to end care in the home. Any family member in the home should have the right to terminate the situation.
Personal care	Can be managed independently or with assistance from family or paid caregivers.
Safety (physical and financial)	Able to phone for help or push button on a wearable emergency alert if alone for periods of time. Home must be free of fall risks, any stairs safely manageable, bathroom with grab bars and other safety measures in place. Aware of solicitation and scamming when left alone.
Medications	Can be independent or with family or caregiver assistance.
Medical care	Family or caregiver take to appointments, or have home-visiting doctor. Search for caregiver who can drive to appointments.

Nutrition	Meals on Wheels or home-delivered foods can continue in some situations. Family typically takes over meal responsibility.
Transportation	Family or caregiver.
Add-on services by others	Having a family member live with you only works if you can leave the home and have some time off from your oversight duties. Either your loved one should be able to remain at home alone for short periods of time or you must be willing to hire sitter services to give you time off. "Day out" programs are another alternative for care during the daytime hours.
Medicare-paid services	Intermittent Medicare visits at no cost after episode of illness, with doctor's order, establishing need for some form of skilled service, and if patient is homebound (nursing, therapy, bath aide). Hospice visits for end-of-life care.
Special considerations	In cases of dementia, observe for tendency to leave the house in an attempt to "go home." If at risk of wandering off, jewelry identifying "dementia" should be worn at all times for safe return to home.
Clues it's no longer working	Family fracturing. Depleting resources (financial or emotional). Patient becoming agitated/upset with host family.

4. INDEPENDENT RETIREMENT COMMUNITY / SENIOR APARTMENT LIVING

When appropriate	Mentally sharp, able to manage personal care, safe from exploitation. Good option when home is no longer physically safe. Apartments are handicapped accessible and enable socialization.
Financial cost	Vary based on facility and geographic area. Some are government sponsored "low-income housing" and provide sliding-scale rates based on income.
Payment sources	Private pay. Government-sponsored programs (typically managed by a local housing authority) can offset some of the cost.
Human resources (family/agent)	Some human resource support needed as most of these communities provide no additional services, only a safe apartment and socialization.
Personal care	None provided by the community. Must be able to manage independently or engage privately hired help.
Safety (physical and financial)	Apartments typically provide more physical safety as they are built with the needs of seniors in mind. Many have emergency call cord. May also need to add a wearable emergency call system for falls.
Medications	Must be independent. Community typically provides no assistance. Family or contracted service can set up medication box system as long as the individual can self-administer from the boxes.
Medical care	Independently go to appointments, have someone else take, or have home-visiting doctor.
Nutrition	Maintain own meals. Able to prepare simple meals. Meals on Wheels or other home-delivered food can be arranged. A few retirement communities have centralized meals.

Transportation	Drives or can utilize other means of transport for groceries and errands.
Add-on services done by others	Housekeeping. Emergency alert system.
Medicare-paid services	Intermittent Medicare visits at no cost after episode of illness with doctor's order, establishing need for some form of skilled service, and if patient is homebound (nursing, therapy, bath aide). Hospice visits for end-of-life care.
Special considerations	When moving in to an independent community, realize it's not final. Another move will be required when need for support increases. Prepare accordingly to hire home caregivers or choose a facility.
Clues it's no longer working	Patient is no longer clean, wearing the same clothes every day, losing weight, inadequate food in the home, house dirty, falls, exploitation.

5. CONTINUING CARE RETIREMENT COMMUNITY (CCRC) = LIFE CARE COMMUNITY

Provides the option to live in one location for your lifetime.
Requires you to enter when healthy and independent.
Pay large entrance fee plus monthly fee.

When appropriate	With most communities, you can enter only when independent. As your needs change, you move to assisted living, dementia care, or skilled nursing on the same campus.
Financial cost	Pay a large fee to enter, anywhere from a hundred thousand to a million dollars for entrance if buying life care. Depending on the contract, most of the entrance fee can be returned to your heirs. There are also monthly fees ($3000-$5000 per month) which may increase as care needs increase. Monthly fees for advanced levels of care are lower than comparable community facilities because the entrance fees help to offset costs.
Payment sources	All private pay. LTC Insurance can begin reimbursing cost when personal care is required.
Human resources (family / agent)	Intermittent, unannounced visits are recommended to monitor care.
Personal care	Care follows the same structure as the varying levels of care already discussed (independent, assisted living, dementia, skilled nursing).
Safety (physical and financial)	All the risks associated with living alone are present during the independent years. However, there is on-site staff available to respond to emergencies. Exploitation from the outside is a risk that needs to be monitored.
Medications	Self when independent. Staff-administered at higher levels of care.

Medical care	Nurse available on campus to respond to emergencies, but there will be a wait time if independent. Can go to community doctor or have visiting doctor in independent apartment. On-site doctors for higher levels of care.
Nutrition	Meals provided by the facility at all levels of care.
Transportation	Transport available for doctor visits. Family or other responsible party should meet for all doctor visits.
Add-on services paid by others	Cost of services will increase as needs change.
Medicare-paid services	After a qualifying hospital stay, the skilled nursing unit should bill Medicare for the period of time the patient qualifies for a rehab stay. Medicare home health services are available in the independent setting.
Special considerations	Modified & fee-for-service contracts also exist, but these are not truly life-care contracts. Be sure you know what you are purchasing. There is no government regulation of the financial solvency of the developers, leaving deposits at risk of being taken by a developer's creditors in the event of bankruptcy.
Clues it's no longer working	This is an option that should last a lifetime. However, it is a large commitment, so do your research and make sure that others in the community are having their needs met as their health declines. Ask others in the community if they are happy there.

6. ASSISTED-LIVING COMMUNITY

*Patients have their own apartments plus
24-hour attendant care available.*

When appropriate	Mentally sharp or early stage of memory loss. Able to manage most of personal care. Independent toileting. Aware of needs, knows when to ask for help.
Financial cost	Cost varies based on facility, apartment size, and services. At time of publication, current US average for a room is $3600 monthly. Many are cost structured like a cafeteria plan: Added services cost more per option chosen. When going in, inquire about starting cost and what the maximum cost would be with all services.
Payment sources	Private pay. Long-term care insurance (LTC) will usually pay if you are receiving personal-care assistance. VA pension for some veterans and their widow(er)s.
Human resources (family/agent)	In a well-run facility, family involvement is only needed for emergencies. However, it is always advisable to make visits to monitor patient status.
Personal care	Varying levels of personal care available. The patient must be able to wait their turn for care, so this type of facility is best suited for patients who can toilet independently or wear diapers. Additional care services can be purchased for bathing, dressing, night care, transport to dining room for meals.
Safety (physical and financial)	Emergency call cords in apartments. May also need to add a wearable emergency call system for falls. There can be varying licenses for these facilities. Some communities require patients be able to evacuate independently in an emergency; others can assist evacuation.
Medications	Can be independent or the facility can manage & administer all medications (for an additional monthly fee).

Medical care	Independently go to appointments, have someone else take, or have home-visiting doctor. Typically, a nurse is on site during business hours Monday through Friday. Other hours, the facility is staffed with unlicensed care staff.
Nutrition	Meals provided by the facility in a community dining room. If unable to get to meals independently, meal transport is available, usually for an additional fee.
Transportation	Most facilities provide van transportation to doctors and shopping.
Add-on services done by others	Housekeeping provided at no charge. Most also do a load of laundry weekly when they change bed linens and wash towels. Additional laundry services usually at an additional fee. Many patients hire personal caregivers in addition to facility staff in an attempt to remain where they are.
Medicare-paid services	Intermittent Medicare visits at no cost after episode of illness, with doctor's order establishing need for some form of skilled service, and if patient is home-bound (nursing, therapy, bath aide). Hospice visits for end-of-life care.
Special considerations	A confused patient who would walk out of the facility and get lost is not appropriate for assisted living except in a memory care unit—see secured dementia care facility below. Depending on the type of license the facility holds, the patient may need to move when they can no longer evacuate independently in an emergency. You need to know this in advance. Most facilities allow patients to decline over time and remain in the same apartment with additional support services added on.
Clues it's no longer working	Patient not doing well due to either a poorly run facility or their needs surpassing what the facility can manage. If continuous nursing care is needed beyond business hours, then it may be time to move.

7. SECURED DEMENTIA-CARE FACILITY

*Special facility that protects the patient from wandering
out and getting lost or hurt. Locked facility. Staff are trained in
dementia care. Most also have safe outdoor walking area.
Many assisted-living facilities have attached dementia units,
making this combination a great option.*

When appropriate	When patients walk independently and are at risk to leave. Other patients need this specialized care because of dementia agitation. They require staff who are skilled in redirecting them when upset and staff who can comfort their fears.
Financial cost	Varies greatly based on geography. Average cost is about $5000 monthly. This is considerably higher than assisted living but the cost is more stable over time (less add-on costs as more care is needed).
Payment sources	Private pay. Rarely, Medicaid. Long-term care insurance. VA pension for some veterans and their widow(er)s.
Human resources (family/agent)	Intermittent visits to monitor care / patient status. Otherwise, needed for emergencies.
Personal care	All personal care delivered as needed.
Safety (physical and financial)	These are some of the safest facilities in terms of physical well-being. No money should go into the facility with the patient, so minimal financial risk.
Medications	Administered by staff.
Medical care	Most have a doctor group who does on-site visits. To leave for doctor visits or to see a specialist would be the responsibility of family. Most have a licensed nurse on duty during business hours and on call after hours.

Nutrition	Meals provided by the facility.
Transportation	Responsibility of the family.
Add-on services done by others	No additional fees unless they charge extra for adult diapers or nutritional supplements.
Medicare-paid services	Intermittent Medicare visits at no cost after episode of illness, with doctor's order establishing need for some form of skilled service, and if patient is home-bound (nursing, therapy, bath aide). Hospice visits for end-of-life care.
Special considerations	Understand the environment and don't send your loved one there with items of value. Patients often "share" personal belongings and wander into each other's rooms, taking what they want. Find out from the start if your loved one can remain for the rest of their life. Most will allow this with hospice services toward end-of-life.
Clues it's no longer working	At the start it will feel as though it is not working. The vast majority of patients don't understand or acknowledge the need for placement. They simply know they are upset and not home. Read the chapter on dementia to better understand. Allow three to six months before making any decisions to move. Once the patient is no longer a wander risk and no longer having difficult behaviors, they can be moved if needed. However, moves are especially disrupting for dementia patients, so proceed with great caution and only with good reason.

8. RESIDENTIAL CARE HOMES = BOARD & CARE HOMES = PERSONAL CARE HOMES (PCH)

These are private homes in residential neighborhoods,
staffed with caregivers who may or may not be licensed depending
on the state and number of patients who live in the home.
Some unlicensed facilities are operating illegally but are tolerated
for lack of alternatives. Some of the best & worst care is in PCHs.
Scrupulous reference checks are imperative.

When appropriate	With the right ownership and management, most patients can live safely in a care home for the long term. The exceptions are patients who may wander off and get lost, or those with a high level of agitation as they can easily upset other patients in the house. Additionally, patients who require continuous nursing care aren't appropriate.
Financial cost	Varies greatly based on geography and size. Average cost is about $3000 monthly. Once needs are assessed and rate determined, monthly care cost stays more constant than assisted living (fewer add-on costs).
Payment sources	Private pay. In rare circumstances, Medicaid may pay. Long-term care insurance would be on a case-by-case basis.
Human resources (family/agent)	Recommend family oversight with unannounced visits. Since these are smaller homes with limited supervision, frequent checking is prudent. Care varies significantly depending on the caregiver on duty. Observe closely until a comfort level is achieved.
Personal care	Make sure to find out if there are limits on personal care. Most do everything.
Safety (physical and financial)	As long as the environment is free of fall risks and bathrooms are handicapped accessible, safety is not generally a concern. Smaller homes are not required to have sprinkler systems installed for fire. No money or valuables should go with the patient.

Medications	Administered by staff.
Medical care	Most have a doctor group for home visits. To leave for doctor visits or to see a specialist would be the responsibility of family. Any nursing needs handled by intermittent Medicare visits. Rare PCHs have nurse owners.
Nutrition	Meals provided by the facility.
Transportation	Responsibility of the family.
Add-on services	No additional fees unless they charge extra for adult diapers or supplements.
Medicare-paid services	Intermittent Medicare visits at no cost after episode of illness, with doctor's order establishing need for some form of skilled service, and if patient is home-bound (nursing, therapy, bath aide). Hospice visits for end-of-life care.
Special considerations	Most are calm environments with minimum stimulation. This works well for some patients who enjoy quiet. This can be a wonderful long-term solution; remaining until the end-of-life is the norm. Just don't forget to monitor care.
Clues it's no longer working	Patient not doing well either due to a poorly run facility or their needs surpassing what the facility can manage. There is typically a decision point to see if more medical care is desired or if hospice care is the preferred path. For more medical care, move to a nursing facility. Hospice care can be delivered in the home.

9. NURSING FACILITY (NF) – LONG-TERM NURSING CARE

Can be for short-term rehabilitation or long-term custodial care.
Be prepared as these are homes to patients with varying levels
of physical and mental impairments.

When appropriate	After an inpatient hospital stay, patients who meet requirements can be admitted under Medicare payment for rehabilitation. Medicare pays for a limited time. Then, the patient can leave or may be able to remain long term. With a Medicare stay, discharge plans need to start right away because of Medicare time limits.
	Admission that is not following a hospitalization and simply based on a growing need for more care can be less complicated. Dementia patients without highly agitated behaviors or wander risk are also appropriate for nursing facility care.
Financial cost	See Medicare paid services below. Average monthly cost for long-term nursing facility care is just under $7000 nationally. Medicare and Medicaid pay for a semi-private room, so your loved one may be sharing a room unless you privately pay to upgrade to a single room.
Payment sources	Medicare and supplement for the initial period of rehab after a qualifying hospitalization. Private pay. LTC Insurance. Medicaid if qualify financially and medically. VA pension for some veterans and their widow(er)s.
Human resources (family/agent)	Need to stay closely engaged during a Medicare stay as plans are needed for what comes next. From the start, find out if staying long-term is an option or not. Additional work may be required for next steps. Long-term, make unannounced visits at varying times of the day, night, and weekends are best.
Personal care	All personal care delivered as needed.

Safety (physical and financial)	One of the biggest risks is confusion after hospitalization which can lead to falls. No money or valuables should go to the facility with the patient.
Medications	Administered by staff.
Medical care	Nurses on site 24 hours a day. Doctors visit. Van transport may be available for community doctor visits. Family must meet at the appointment.
Nutrition	Meals provided by the facility.
Transportation	Most have transport available for doctor visits or family can take.
Add-on services	No additional fees during Medicare days. After that, there is a daily fee, cost of medications, disposable supplies (adult diapers, wipes, etc.).
Medicare-paid services	Medicare stay: cost fully paid by Medicare the first 20 days. After that there is a daily copay for up to a total of 100 days for as many days that you qualify under Medicare regulations (skilled care being medically beneficial). Few patients meet medical criteria for the full 100 days.
Special considerations	Know you need to have a plan in place from the start as to where you go next. If funds are limited and you will be trying to qualify your family member for a long-term Medicaid-paid bed, then it is best to begin the rehab stay in a facility where a Medicaid bed is an option. This avoids another move. You may need a case manager and / or Medicaid elder-law attorney to assist with Medicaid.
Clues it's no longer working	Sometimes, elderly patients are admitted to SNF rehab and are unwilling or unable to put the effort in to make rehab progress. This will shorten the time Medicare will reimburse for the stay. Remain in close touch with the SNF staff (usually the social worker) to have a sense when Medicare days will end. The silver lining of these stays is that it can give you an inside look at a nursing facility to determine if this might be a good option long term for your loved one.

Overwhelmed? It's not surprising if you are. For that reason, the following table provides a snapshot of placement alternatives, both for the acute medical stage and for long-term care, along with payment information for each level of care.

PLACEMENT ALTERNATIVES – LEVEL OF CARE AND PAYMENT OPTIONS

*A. Utilize all medical care in acute stage of illness to achieve
maximum wellness first. Then move on to consider
Long-term Placement Options*

Location	Average Stay	Type of Care/ Information	Payment
Hospital (acute)	3-5 days	Acute episode of illness.	Medicare, Medicaid, Insurance
Rehab hospital (acute)	2-3 weeks	Must tolerate 3 hours per day of therapy (physical, occupational, speech).	Medicare, Medicaid, Insurance
Long-term acute hospital care (LTAC)	3-4 weeks	Too ill for nursing home. Too weak for rehab. Qualify for long-term hospital stay.	Medicare, Insurance, Medicaid
Skilled nursing facility (SNF)	3-5 weeks (max 100 days)	Skilled care needed (therapy or nursing) as long as medically necessary up to 100 days.	Medicare, Insurance. Need three-day inpatient hospital stay to qualify.
Assisted living (for recovery)	Variable	Independent for part of the time. Help needed for care, meals, medications.	Private pay. Can extend stay as long as able to pay.
Home health care (skilled)	Usually 4-8 weeks	Therapy or nursing as long as care is intermittent, skilled need, doctor ordered, and patient is homebound.	Medicare, Insurance, Medicaid to a limited degree.

B. Once Medicare quits paying—
long-term care / non-medical options for long term

Location	Type of Care / Information	Payment
Nursing home (long-term care)	Must meet medical necessity threshold to qualify for Medicaid & LTC Ins. Need 2 ADLs or severe cognitive impairment. Should be medically stable.	Private pay, LTC Ins., Medicaid with financial qualification. VA pension.
Assisted living (residential)	Able to stay alone part-time. Help with care, meals, and medications as needed.	Private pay. LTC Ins. Very few Medicaid beds. VA pension.
Dementia facility (long-term care)	Care needed for cognitive reasons. May be wander risk so locked facility required.	Private pay. LTC Ins. Few Medicaid beds. VA pension.
Personal care (residential) home	Private home. Unlicensed caregiver available at all times.	Private pay. Very few Medicaid beds.
Hospice	Life expectancy six months or less. Intermittent visits in the home or a facility.	Medicare. Medicaid. Insurance.
Hourly non-medical care at home	Hourly care can cover brief or extended hours of care.	Private pay. LTC Ins. Medicaid if qualify. VA pension.
Family care at home	Don't try to do 100%. Have respite coverage for time away.	FMLA to hold job and care by family.

Regarding placement, here is the good news: Options for care continue to flourish. The bad news is that it can be confusing and costly. Time and research are required. For your loved one, you're choosing not just a facility but a home. So once you've narrowed options down to a short list, look for qualities of home as you walk through places you've chosen to evaluate. But what if you don't have a short list? How do you decide which facilities to evaluate? Where to go?

Take it step by step. Help is at hand if you seek out families with experience; doctors, case managers, and friends who have been in similar situations can help in deciding where to go. If finances allow, consider an independent assessment by a knowledgeable professional in the community prior to placement. But make sure they're not being paid a *placement fee* from the facility for admission as that can color their recommendations. You want an endorsement with no financial bias.

Your evaluation should be twofold: What level of care does the patient need and what facilities would best meet the needs? In addition, always ask about employee turnover. If an organization changes staff constantly, cross it off your list, since staff fluctuations generally unsettle patients and undermine quality. As noted in Chapter 14, staff must *know* the patient in order to give optimal care, tailored for that specific individual. For an amazing amount of information on nursing homes, go to Nursing Home Compare at www.medicare.gov/nursinghomecompare/search.html.

Similar sites exist for assisted-living facilities (with less information) on state government-specific websites. Also check out the website of your local Area Agency on Aging (AAA).

One last item of *really good news* has to do with the impact of care expenses on your tax return. These documented expenses usually are tax-deductible as medical expenses. Providing data to your accountant can dramatically reduce the total tax burden. With the emotional drain of this stage and these painful decisions, it's nice to have a *silver lining.*

~ LESSON ~

Options for care are plentiful, but look before you leap. Consider what will best serve your loved one for a length of time before deciding. An elder-care attorney can assist with finances and benefits. As you visit facilities during your search, remain skeptical, realizing that promises may not be kept, and that every facility wants its beds fully occupied and profitable. An independent evaluation with recommendations may minimize mistakes. After all, moving is costly, wearing, and destabilizing, so you want to avoid do-overs.

The final chapter looks at the ultimate gift we can give ourselves and our family—*The Blueprint to Age Your Way.* This allows us all to document our lives, our plans, our fears.

CHAPTER EIGHTEEN

The Blueprint to Age Your Way

Beyond Conversation

The Blueprint to Age Your Way is what our family
uses for our annual review.

The Importance of a Written Plan

Go beyond conversation to give your plan staying power. Yes, conversation is invaluable for thinking out loud and crystalizing your beliefs. But the spoken word is subject to interpretation and memory. Details evaporate, especially when stress enters the picture. The responsible party can change or even die. At that point, sibling feuds erupt when one claims, "Mom told me what she really wanted," and the other says, "Your word against mine." That's why your plan must be in writing and in an organized, accessible format. It can preserve peace in the family, as well as your own peace of mind.

Because our lives have both unrelated and interdependent parts, our planning should too. Taken as a whole, it can seem overwhelming, so give yourself permission to divide the work into manageable chunks. As you view your journey down the road of aging, you may feel sad or frightened. Parts of the planning process may be tedious or confusing. We all have so many layers to our lives! But to be realistic, these challenges should motivate you. If pulling together the numerous parts of your life is daunting for you, just think how hard it would be for someone else. Don't leave it to them.

Once you've completed your plan, then it's time to meet with your responsible party or family. Share your documented life guide, a precious compilation. Then ask all parties to commit to meeting yearly for review, sooner if you make significant changes. The same format you used originally can be followed for amendments which makes the hill easier to climb each year. Remember, this is a gift for both you and your family. It's worth your time, worth your focus. Below are the broad categories you'll cover.

MEDICAL

This section is where my heart fully resides, since so often in my career I have touched the pain of passivity and the power of planning. Your voice can be heard and your wishes followed when you take the right steps. This aspect of planning calls for medical expertise. Seek a guide with clinical background—a doctor, nurse practitioner, physician's assistant, geriatrician, or nurse. In order to make sound decisions, you need to know and understand your alternatives. In the past, people became ill, aged, and died of natural causes. This is no longer the case. We have options to intervene, changing or delaying nature's cycle. That's why you must document your wishes point-by-point. Before you get sick, it's easier to get inside your own head, determine your individual philosophy of life, death, and illness. Legal documents are broad; your plan is best followed by means of written specifics.

The clinical guide person you choose should have the broadest possible experience, both inpatient and outpatient. All decisions have implications to be considered, details to be explained. Don't select an option without understanding how this would impact your day-to-day life. There are no right or wrong choices, merely what best defines the way you want to live your life.

To find your medical helper, a good place to start is with your primary care physician, his or her nurse, a home-health nurse, or medical case manager who takes this role seriously. Along with making sure the person has a suitable resume, ask the question—do they *really listen* to *you*? Will they spend enough time to ensure you completely understand and document your options? Networking in your community is another excellent approach. Or, you can search web-based sources for geriatric care managers or case managers.

A comprehensive medical plan should include these written documents:

- *My Mobile Demo* (defined below)

- Other medical documents

- Medical and prescription cards, photo ID

- *Medical Planning Worksheet* (defined below)

- Setting of priorities

- List of your favorites, what you truly enjoy

- List of fears

- Concessions you are willing to make when needed

- Preference for CPR

As you read through specifics, it will become clear how important this is. No matter what system you use, it is vital to implement a *My Mobile Demo* (demographics) record. This condenses critical data about you into a single document: Medical conditions, medications, emergency contacts, doctors, and more. Not only is the format efficient, it also improves medical care. But it works only when the data is current, concise, and comprehensive. When time is of the essence, the document can speak for you and quickly inform emergency services or other medical personnel of everything they need to know at a glance. Then they can focus on treating your current problem. Hundreds of times I've seen this condensed format work in a way that expedites needed care. It is a must for everyone.

In my life as a nurse case manager, we called 911 many times for patient emergencies. The minute EMS arrived and we handed them the condensed medical demographics, the reaction was always the same: Visible relief. After a brief moment for review, they could go straight to work, managing the emergency. No wasted time.

The *Medical Planning Worksheet* helps you walk through decision points that might be encountered down the road. It lists both short-term and long-term interventions. All these are your choices to make along the way. The worksheet serves as a reference for your surrogate decision maker if you are unable to communicate. Even when you're unable to talk, these become your stated wishes and should be followed.

The priorities and favorites documents are a marvelous resource for others involved in your life. I can't even begin to count the number of times I wanted this information on my patients, but they were beyond their time to speak. Taking a wild guess at what brings joy to someone else is such a hollow feeling. Some patients say they're terrified of dying alone. Others worry that they won't be able to look out a window. These nuggets of knowledge are powerful: If you're the patient, you can rest assured that your intimate worries will be taken into account, and, if you're the patient's family, you'll be better able to ease your loved one's final chapter.

"You can't always get what you want," the song lyric goes, which is why your plan must include concessions. It's a medical *plan*, not a medical pipe-dream, so it has to be practical. How many of us have tried to talk a parent out of driving because of safety concerns? We involve doctors, we arrange painful family interventions, we try everything in our power. No luck. That's why the plan includes a list of concessions you'd be willing to make when needed, such as driving, moving out of your home, etc. When topics being discussed seem years or decades away, it's easy to be logical and sign agreements. Then, when the time arrives, the signed commitment holds weight.

Preference for CPR finishes out your plan's medical section. This answers a sensitive question: Does the patient want medical personnel to pursue every possible measure to prolong biological function or does the patient want to allow a *natural death* when their time comes. It's a matter of individual preference; no right and no wrong answers.

PERSONAL

In the event of incapacity or need for help, written information is a gold mine. Who are your closest friends, your clergy, beautician, attorney? The list goes on and on. Even if you organize your contacts on your computer or address book, someone else may have trouble making sense of it. You store so much in your head. Help your helper. Keep this data in your centralized place so someone else could continue your routines with the least disruption.

So many other details to think of. Insurance—what company, broker, types of policies? Household—who cleans, mows the lawn, checks for pests, fixes the plumbing? An often forgotten but extremely important consideration is log-ins, passwords, personal identification numbers (PINs), location of keys. Your advocate's hands will be tied without this information, which is mandatory to access accounts or discontinue service when no longer needed. Years after his death, my father is still cycling around Facebook for lack of his password. The hassles are unending.

It's tempting to ignore funeral planning. Who wants to talk out loud about that? I've lost count of the funerals I have planned. Each one is a personal expression of the individual; traditional burial or cremation, service or not, what funeral home? Ideally you'll have everything predetermined and paid in advance (if funds are available). If funds are not available for pre-payment, then the pre-planning can be done alone. It's inevitable: Someone has to make these choices. If you don't, you're merely dumping it on another person. And there's other data required at the time of death. Veterans need to list their military branch, rank at discharge, enlistment date and location, discharge date and location, service number. Parents' full names and birthplace are to be included. Are there specific items you wish to have listed in your obituary? Do you even *want* an obituary?

This is only the tip of the iceberg. Family may be at a loss to gather and complete everything when there are far greater priorities than hopelessly hunting down data that could have been documented in advance.

LEGAL/VITAL DOCUMENTS

Gathering of legal and other vital documents is extensive. I can't imagine that anyone has all these documents in one location. By centralizing, your family will be able to respond to any legal situation. There are many online options for processing of legal documents. However, an attorney who is familiar with state statutes is worth the investment to assure everything is correct. Ask in your community for lawyer referrals. Satisfied customers are the best guide. Another option is to conduct a web-based search for elder-law or estate-planning attorneys.

A comprehensive plan may include all or part of the list below. Some items may seem silly to you now. But in the long run, they can protect relationships between your loved ones by documenting your wishes unequivocally, leaving little to chance interpretation.

- Medical Power of Attorney

- Durable / Financial Power of Attorney

- Directive to Physician

- Medical Release—HIPAA Release of Information

- Guardianship Designation

- Disposition of Remains

- Will

- Designation of Executor

- Birth Certificates (for you and your children)

- Death Certificate (for your spouse or any children)

- Adoption Papers

- Marriage Certificate

- Divorce Papers

- Pre-nuptial Agreement

- Trust Agreements

- Partnership Agreements

- Tax Returns (or their location)

FINANCIAL

Financial concerns can be a source of consternation, especially if resources are slim, deep, or chaotic. Many people are sensitive about sharing personal financial information. Don't worry: you don't have to reveal specifics. What your family needs to know is the location of resources and where to obtain information should you become incapacitated. Don't saddle them with such tasks as tracking down bank accounts, investments, real estate. What is your income stream and what are your recurring obligations? Be particularly clear about direct deposits and automatic withdrawals.

Your family must know what account receives Social Security and other recurring deposits, such as pension and IRA disbursements. In an attempt to simplify matters, some families move forward quickly to consolidate multiple bank accounts. This can be a drastic mistake. Any account that receives direct deposits must remain open to retain the benefit. If the account that receives your Social Security check is closed, then there is an automatic assumption the individual has died and deposits will automatically cease. With the end of Social Security payments, your Medicare health insurance also ends.

I recall working with a family who innocently made this mistake. It took months of paying privately for doctors, medications, and hospitals until the Medicare was reinstated. Rosanne's grandson, John, was the one who assumed responsibility when her Parkinson's progressed to the point that independence was no longer an option. Rosanne's daughter should have been the designated party, but responsibility had never been her strong-suit. The sad reality was that the daughter was still financially dependent on her mom. Smart Rosanne had skipped over her daughter in naming her grandson as power or attorney. This would have created permanent damage to family relationships, except the daughter needed to stay attached to receive her monthly "allowance."

In trying to juggle his own business, his financially dependent mother, and his declining grandmother, John opted to consolidate bank accounts, closing the account that received Rosanne's Social Security direct deposit. He had no idea of the consequences. Social Security determined she died, stopped her payments, and discontinued her Medicare. This snowballed to her Medicare supplement insurance and prescription coverage being cancelled as well. It took John four months to realize Rosanne was without insurance, but it became acutely obvious when she was hospitalized with no coverage. After $97,000 in medical and prescription expenses to pay, I was called in to help. The tense family situation escalated to new heights. John had to liquidate assets to pay medical bills and his dependent mother's "allowance." We had to wait until Rosanne was well enough to be taken to the Social Security office two months later to prove she was alive. It was humiliating.

Even after that, it took another three months to get all the interrelated systems to reactivate her status to living. Nine months from start to finish. I don't know how long it took Medicare to reimburse the out-of-pocket payments, but I'm sure it wasn't fast.

~ LESSON ~

Never close a bank account without first identifying where retirement benefits are direct-deposited (Social Security, retirement, IRA distributions, etc.). When an account that receives Social Security payments is closed, death is automatically assumed and payments cease, along with associated medical coverage (Medicare). It can take many months to correct this costly and innocent mistake.

In the same way, regular payments to continue your insurance and other obligations must continue or vital safeguards may disappear. The important thing is to equip your responsible party with all the right information to keep you stable.

A solid plan also designates a co-signer on your primary bank account (the one that has a regular source of income) so that your trusted agent can pay bills. In a crisis, you certainly want to ensure the lights stay on.

CENTRALIZE YOUR PLAN

Now that you have a sense of what needs to be gathered and recorded, let's look at accessibility. Everything mentioned in this final chapter should be kept together. A centralized and tabbed three-ring binder allows you to gather, add, and delete items through the years. Life is fluid. A blueprint should be, too. You may wish to duplicate the book, leaving a copy with your responsible party or create a password-protected electronic version.

The person who steps in to assist in a time of crisis will be forever grateful to have a repository of answers. No requirement to spend months of turning your house upside down, digging for the pieces of your life. With the tools at hand, frustration is minimized and focus on your current situation is maximized. That is the ideal goal.

You can be successful in putting together your documented plan in any format that works for you. But, be warned...it takes time, patience, and organization to achieve success. If you operate best with a roadmap, then the *Blueprint to Age Your Way* can be the solution. It is available through www.AgeYourWay.com.

The format for *My Mobile Demo* is a form that can be downloaded to any computer and customized for you. All necessary categories are listed, ready to enter your own information. Every time an item changes, the document is easily updated and printed to be kept in the front section of your blueprint. Destroy any previous versions to avoid confusion. Handing a copy to a medical responder in need of treating you is helpful beyond words. It is made available to you as part of the *Blueprint to Age Your Way.*

~ IN CLOSING ~

The most precious gift we all have is our time, which levels the playing field for everyone, a mere 24 hours in each day. For anyone who has invested their time to read this book, I thank you for your gift of time. I'm honored as it gives me an opportunity to share the passion close to my heart, put it onto the page, and into your thoughts. My gift back to you is the opportunity to document your life guide, a treasure for years to come, peace of mind for you and those you love. The unthinkable is not for you. Happy planning!

Acknowledgments

As a novice writer in my sixties, I have a long list of people to thank for helping this passion become a reality. It's hard to know where to begin.

First, my patients: You have touched my soul in a manner that lingers, long after the physical touch has ended. The lasting feelings, joys, and sorrows are forever etched in my heart. You have all been such a gift. Throughout the years, you have welcomed me into your lives in a way that I cherish and respect. In lockstep with my patients have been their loving families and caregivers who were the difference makers. I marvel at all you willingly give to enrich the lives of our patients. Thank you for allowing me in. For without you, there would be no stories to tell.

For the professionals I have had the honor to work with, I thank you: the judges, attorneys, trust officers, physicians, nurses, social workers, and countless other experts. Because of you, I've grown personally and professionally. Your example and gentle push taught me how to embrace problems with enthusiasm.

For the family of Nurses Case Management, there are too many to thank. To my partners, Jack and Ben, the epitome of ethical business leaders, you are the greatest treasure my company received. To Catherine and Gary, your willingness to take over the daily reins allowed the company to grow and soar. To the nursing and operations staff, I am in awe of all you accomplish as a cohesive team that continues to always put the patients first.

To those of you who did the hand-holding necessary to take me through the crash course of writing and publishing, I'm in awe of you. Janica, Dennis, Marti, Sylvia, Tami, and Monica: both your patience and guidance are beyond description. Starting out with the A-Team the first time out was a stroke of luck and a true blessing.

To my numerous *first readers*, I'll be forever grateful for your encouragement and your unabashed honesty. Each of you provided gems that allowed me to grasp the reader's perspective. A few of you volunteered more time than I had the right to expect. You know who you are: Alex, Andy, Brent, and Clyde. Thank you for opening my eyes in so many vital areas.

To my family, you are the world to me. Our three children have surpassed our greatest hopes and dreams, much of which is due to the remarkable spouses they chose. It is a gift to love and admire the six of you. I marvel at your ability to juggle all you do while demonstrating grace under pressure. Our eight grandchildren are the ultimate reward, the promise of a glorious future.

And to my Hank, my heartbeat, my soulmate, the best husband and father in the world, words are inadequate to express my feelings. Sharing life with you has been the best thing that ever happened. Partnering with you in the publishing was icing on the cake. Together we stumbled through the process, knowing little, laughing much, and welcoming the journey of learning what to do next. The humor and delight you brought into our lives many years ago continues to this very day. You are my most precious goofball.

About the Author

DEBBIE PEARSON has worked as a nurse for forty years. Credentials include a Bachelor of Science in Nursing, Nationally Certified Case Manager, Aging Life Care Professional, and Texas Certified Guardian. She founded Nurses Case Management in 2000, which became the ultimate method of serving in the role of patient advocate.  Her lifelong commitment to "patient first" has guided her years of caring and has culminated in the writing of *Age Your Way.*

Index

Page numbers in *italics* mark the locations of photos.

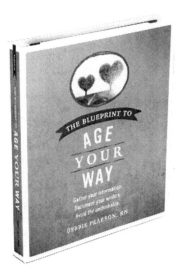

The Blueprint to Age Your Way is a comprehensive system designed to help you organize and record vital legal, financial and medical information and document your unique wishes for living and dying. Completion of the blueprint quiets the chaos, providing certainty and peace of mind.

When aging, injury or illness robs us of the ability to make our own decisions, crucial choices about how we will live and ultimately die — that we may have to live with for decades — can be left to other people. This can be tragic for the aging person and traumatic for the loved ones who are asked to make critical decisions without a foundation of information.

Author Debbie Pearson, RN designed *The Blueprint to Age Your Way* to make sure that doesn't happen. This companion piece to the book *Age Your Way* includes all the tools you need to create a personal plan that will clarify your preferences and provide the documentation essential to executing your strategy, including:

- All necessary legal, financial and medical documents
- A record of your priorities, favorites and fears
- Wishes for ongoing health care and end-of-life choices
- Care and placement preferences
- Funeral and burial wishes and special bequests
- And more...

With this Blueprint as your guide, your personal plan will fill the void, leaving no question about available resources and unique wishes for both living and dying, providing both you and your loved ones with the ultimate gift—peace of mind.

Visit **www.AgeYourWay.com/blueprint** today
to order your *Blueprint to Age Your Way* organizer.

CPSIA information can be obtained
at www.ICGtesting.com
Printed in the USA
FFOW05n2016300816